Closer to God

The Ultimate Adventure!

Henry Jacob Rupp MD

D1445738

CLOSER TO GOD
The Ultimate Adventure!

ISBN: 9798709843202

Dedication

This book is dedicated to Sandy, my wife and best friend, and to you the reader. The <u>Ultimate Adventure</u> has just begun as each of us draw <u>Closer To God</u>. We look forward to spending eternity together with you.

Acknowledgments

Special appreciation to Sandy, my wife and best friend, who edited my book after spending many lonely nights while I was writing. (Now it's her turn to write a book.) Thanks to our friend, Jan Seever, and new friend Kathy Haasdyk, for patient proofreading. Thanks to new friend Cindy Buckshon, who formatted the book and advised us on the final stages. And finally, thanks to our favorite artist, Theresa Hertling, who helped create the cover design. We are so grateful to each of you for your expert assistance. What would we do without our friends?

Adventure
or
Relationship?!? Game Show?

CLOSER TO GOD: The Ultimate Adventure!

Growing closer to God is the ultimate adventure! Nothing else can compare. God promises that if we "draw closer to Him, He will draw closer to us." (James 4:8)

? When
How
Why!

The place to start is right where you are! When you become a follower of Jesus, you will find "inexpressible and glorious joy." (I Peter 1:8) But that is just the beginning of the adventure. God's "infinite love" is beyond our wildest imagination. He will draw closer at whatever rate we draw to Him. You may choose to inch closer or walk at a brisk pace.

Amazingly, God tells us that our journey will never end. He promises that it will continue at His right hand, where there are pleasures forever. (Psalm 16:11 AMP) Jesus tells us: "My Father's house has many rooms, and I am going there to prepare a place for you. I will come back and take you to be with me where I am." (John 14:2,3) Our ultimate adventure will be very close to God and will never end.

Each chapter of this book will help you grow closer to God. There are pits to avoid, which are mentioned from time to time. Most importantly, move toward God's love with all your heart, mind, and strength. As you grow closer to God, His glory, wisdom, and power will thrill your anticipation for more adventure.

Read on!

Not a base/foundation concept to most!

Bold statement

Contents

Why Write This Book?

"Of books, there is no end," so why write this one? Here is my reason: I would like to write about interesting new issues. I hope that many of these thoughts are unique, ones that you haven't considered before. However, a much more important reason to write this book is so you grow closer to the Lord. That is huge! *JRS "up."*

How close can you and I get to the Lord? If we are talking inches closer, that's okay, but it is a bit minimal. What if, after reading this book, you go from being the doorman at heaven's entrance to the doorman at the throne room? There, when you open the throne room door, the love that radiates out is unbelievable! Draw nearer to God for incredible rewards. Keep on reading; your "closeness to the Lord" is at stake!

Draw near to God, and he will draw near to you. (James 4:8) *JRV plaque*

Those who are far from you will perish; but as for me, it is good to be near God. (Psalm 73:27,28)

And without faith, it is impossible to please him, for whoever would draw near to God must believe that he exists and that he rewards those who seek him. (Hebrews 11:6)

"You will seek me and find me when you seek me with all your heart. I will be found by you," declares the Lord. (Jeremiah 29:13,14)

Let us draw near to God with a sincere heart and with the full assurance that faith brings. (Hebrews 10:22)

The Sword of the Spirit

The sword of the Spirit is the Word of God, and it is very powerful. We Christians will do best if we use the blade very carefully. How are you doing wielding the sword of God's Word? One never knows when the sword is needed. Don't go into the battle of life without it. Of the six pieces of the armor of God, the sword is the only offensive weapon. However, I suspect in a crisis; you could push at evil with the shield of faith or smash evil with your helmet of salvation. It's just better to have God's Word, the sword, available. Here is a quick lesson regarding how to use the sword of the Spirit.

First of all, it helps to memorize the Word of God, which is the sword, so it is available at all times. If you can't remember a verse exactly, use your "paraphrased" version. The Holy Spirit can pray through you powerfully even if your personal sword is not so sharp!

Second, it is tempting to swing, swing, swing the sword, and fire out verse after verse in the spiritual battle. Careful fighters, however, wait for the best moment and thrust with one perfect verse into the heart of the matter instead of chopping at a knee cap or toe. The Holy Spirit can help you to find the Word or message that will win the battle.

The third challenge is to use the sword in love. Your goal is to pierce evil, but you are to walk away better friends than you were before the joust. That sounds impossible, but God's love, compassion, and mercy should be present when using God's Word. Use the sword of the Word to bring others "CLOSER TO GOD."

Here are some helpful hints on using the sword of the Spirit, the Word of God. Many people are quite happy to talk with you about their troubles. After silently praying, you might ask them if it would be okay if you prayed about their problem. Most people are so glad for you to pray for them. Gently add the Scripture into your prayer. Here's an example prayer: The Bible says to "ask, and you will receive" so Lord I ask you to be with _____ and help him/her deal with this problem of _____.

won't look up!

Here are some Word Swords:

- For health problems, pray healing verses: (Isaiah 53:5, Psalm 103:2,3)
- For worry/anxiety problems, pray: (Philippians 4:6,7, Matthew 6:25-34)
- For fear, pray the fear verses: (2 Timothy 1:7, Joshua 1:9)
- money problems, pray the money verses: (John 10:10, Philippians 4:19)
- If it's a beautiful sunset, exclaim that the heavens are declaring God's Glory and pouring out speech about God. (Psalm 19:1, Psalm 8)

I know you get the picture. Memorize and practice swinging the sword of the Spirit, which is God's Word. Then pray that the Holy Spirit will pierce that person's heart with love to the Lord as your prayer is answered. Your sword is meant to draw them CLOSER TO GOD, the Ultimate Adventure.

I have tried to put simple verses below each sword so that you will see them often and memorize the ones you might need in your next spiritual battle.

For the word of God is alive and powerful. It is sharper than the sharpest two-edged sword, cutting between soul and spirit, joint and marrow. It exposes our innermost thoughts and desires. (Hebrews 4:12)

Therefore put on the full armor of God. Stand firm with the belt of truth, the breastplate of righteousness, your feet with the gospel of peace, the shield of faith, the helmet of salvation, and the SWORD of the SPIRIT, which is the WORD of GOD. (Ephesians 6:13-17, my caps)

Do your best to present yourself to God as one approved, who correctly handles the word of truth. (2 Timothy 2:15)

Ask, and it will be given to you; seek, and you will find; knock, and the door will be opened to you. (Matthew 7:7)

I can do everything through Christ, who gives me strength. (Philippians 4:13 NLT)

And my God will meet all your needs according to the riches of his glory in Christ Jesus. (Philippians 4:19)

 **Notes for reflection**

Spo verse 2021

The Great Sadness

"JP"?

There is "the great sadness" that many of us carry each day of our lives. One of my friend's sadness is the senseless drowning of his teenage son, another a painful suicide, another was a friend whose husband was crushed under his car one day after he retired. The great sadness hurts each day. It is a great sadness. — SAY DiFFeReNTly!

For some, it might be no spouse or children, illness, abuse, or divorce. For others, it might be the inability to forgive someone or even forgive God who didn't intervene. Many bear it quietly, silently; it seems like a great grayness. Do you carry a great sadness?

It is possible that your sadness may work toward great good in your life! Here are powerful verses for anyone with great sorrow. Ask the Holy Spirit to use His Word as a sword to slash away at your great sadness.

Better words

Better words

We know that in all things, God works for the good of those who love him, who have been called according to his purpose. (Romans 8:28)

For our light and momentary troubles are achieving for us an eternal glory that far outweighs them all. (2 Corinthians 4:17)

Consider it pure joy, my brothers and sisters, whenever you face trials of many kinds, so that you may be mature and complete, not lacking anything. (James 1:2,4)

And without faith, it is impossible to please God because anyone who comes to him must believe that he exists and that he rewards those who earnestly seek him. (Hebrews 11:6)

Rejoice in the Lord always. I will say it again: Rejoice! (Philippians 4:4)

I know those verses may not completely remove the sadness from you, but they do give hope and a purpose for the sadness by faith. The famous Jesus Prayer: "Lord Jesus, Son of God, have mercy on me a sinner" is an excellent place to start when dealing with the great sadness.

My best solution is to become very, very small with humility, and ask for mercy. That helps me. Then I pray to have God become very, very big with His overwhelming love aimed right at me. I prayerfully stay in that wonderful place as long as I can. As I get smaller, and He gets bigger, then NOTHING ELSE REALLY MATTERS!

Notes for reflection

+ LIKE BUT NOT UNIVERSAL

Is Planet Earth Important?

"quote from?" *"JP"*

Where is the earth on God's "continuum of importance"? Scientists estimate that there are two trillion galaxies and 1×10^{24} stars. That means that there are more stars than all the grains of sand on planet earth! God has created so much. How important is little planet earth to God when He's created all those massive galaxies, stars, and planets?

Are we at the center of His attention, or are we only an insignificant speck of dust in creation? So here is the question: How important is earth to God?

*

Not important_____Very Important

God has told us the answer to that question, and it is excellent news. God's beautiful earth is a stunning work of creation beyond our understanding. God wants us to know that we, on planet earth, are the center of His attention. He has proven that by sending His Son to die for us on earth! Jesus' death and the beautiful world God has created for us are crucial evidence that we are very important in His eyes. Praising Him is our privileged role for all eternity!

In the beginning, God created the heavens and the earth. (Genesis 1:1)

Lift up your eyes on high, and see who has created these things. He calls them all by name. By the greatness of His might and the strength of His power, not one is missing. (Isaiah 40:26)

The heavens declare the glory of God; the skies proclaim the work of his hands. Day after day, they pour forth speech; night after night, they reveal knowledge. (Psalm 19:1,2)

I made the earth and created man on it; it was my hands that stretched out the heavens. (Isaiah 45:12)

Since the creation of the world, God's invisible qualities—his eternal power and divine nature —have been clearly seen, being understood from what has been made, so that people are without excuse. (Romans 1:20)

Thus says God, the Lord, who created the heavens and stretched them out, who spread out the earth and what comes from it, who gives breath to the people on it and spirit to those who walk in it. (Isaiah 42:5 ESV)

For God so loved the world that he gave his one and only Son, that whoever believes in him shall not perish but have eternal life. (John 3:16)

 Notes for reflection

How Important are Humans?

[handwritten: Better Analogy]

Where do humans fit on God's "continuum of importance"? Scientists estimate 8.7 million species of animals exist, and we humans are just one species. Humans are at the top of the food chain because God made it that way. God created us in His image; He gives each of us a spiritual soul so we will live forever! That is amazing. We are at the top of God's animal creations! *[handwritten: Animal]*

How important are you compared to all the other humans that have ever lived? One-half of the people that have ever lived are alive right now. Therefore, if the earth's population is 7 1/2 billion, 15 billion people have lived since the world's creation. You are competing with 15 billion other people for God's attention. *[handwritten: "JP" WHAT]* *[handwritten margin: For Evolutionists / Evolutionists]*

God has "Good News" for each one of us. He hand-picked and chose us individually and destined us for good works, which He has planned from the beginning of time. God has the very hair on our head numbered, and He knows even our thoughts. Furthermore, we will spend eternity living in His place with Him. You and I practice our "personal relationship" with Jesus each day in our prayer time. *[handwritten: write / compared / Better]*

Finally, true love is often determined by how much pain one will endure for another. Jesus' painful death proves His love for each one of us. In summary, God sent His Son to prove we are unique and loved and even wants us to live with Him. Our relationship will not be distant but very close!

The Lord is clear in His message to each one of us. We each are important beyond our wildest expectation on God's "Continuum of Importance!'

[handwritten: " ?, " JP . REALLY]

Not important_____Very Important ✱

So God created mankind in his own image; in the image of God, he created them; male and female, he created them. (Genesis 1:27)

For God so loved the world that he gave his one and only Son, that whoever believes in him shall not perish but have eternal life. (John 3:16)

"For I know the plans I have for you," declares the Lord, "plans to prosper you and not to harm you, plans to give you hope and a future." (Jeremiah 29:11)

For we are God's handiwork, created in Christ Jesus to do good works, which God prepared in advance for us to do. (Ephesians 2:10)

And even the very hairs of your head are all numbered, so don't be afraid. (Matthew 10:30,31)

For the joy set before him, he endured the cross, scorning its shame, and sat down at the right hand of the throne of God. (Hebrews 12:2)

My Father's house has many rooms; I am going there to prepare a place for you? I will come back and take you to be with me that you also may be where I am. (John 14:2,3)

Surely your goodness and love will follow me all the days of my life, and I will dwell in the house of the Lord forever. (Psalm 23:6)

You will fill me with joy in your presence, with eternal pleasures at your right hand. (Psalm 16:11)

 Notes for reflection

Today is at Least a $500 Day!

How much is a human life worth per year? In theory, a year of human life is priceless. According to Wikipedia, in the USA, one human life is worth $9.1 million, and the value of one year of life is $50,000 (the "dialysis standard") to $129,000 per year of quality life."

Health economists suggest that each year is $200,000 and each day is $500; let's go with that higher value. Today is 24 hours long, so that means the value of each hour is $22.83. If you sleep for seven hours, you have used up $160 of your $500 value. "Ethics specialists" seem unable to determine how much one day of life is worth. One day for a patient in hospital Intensive care costs thousands of dollars. Many medical treatments can be tremendously expensive per day.

It may be relatively easy for us to take each day for granted. Here is my solution: imagine that you have to pay $500 in cash upfront for each day of your life! That will help you treasure each moment. Each day of life is not guaranteed; each one is valuable. Treasure the precious day that you are experiencing right now. This next hour has a price tag of $22.83 and is a precious commodity.

For one thing, you could give this hour a fantastic eternal value if you pray in it. If you do that, you have just laid up treasure in Heaven! If any energy is left over, love your neighbor with a touch of Godly love. That turns a $22 hour into "gold" in heaven! We each are so fortunate to be alive today. Don't forget; it's a $500 day!

Give us today our daily bread. (Matthew 6:11)

Rejoice in the Lord always. I will say it again: Rejoice! The Lord is near. (Philippians 4:4-9)

But store up for yourselves treasures in heaven, where moths and vermin do not destroy, where thieves do not break in and steal. (Matthew 6:20)

I tell you, now is the time of God's favor, now is the day of salvation. (2 Corinthians 6:2)

And do this, understanding the present time: The hour has already come for you to wake up from your slumber because our salvation is nearer now than when we first believed. (Romans 13:11)

One person considers one day more sacred than another; another considers every day alike. Whoever regards one day as special does so to the Lord. (Romans 14:5a,6a)

Therefore, we do not lose heart. Though outwardly we are wasting away, yet inwardly we are being renewed day by day. (2 Corinthians 4:16)

 Notes for reflection

The Throne of God

Imagine you are in the throne room of God. It would tell us so much about God if we could zoom up there and look at the throne with its plush seat and armrests. Is it placed on a thick red carpet? How soft is the seat cushion? Headrest? Are there lots of diamonds beautifully set for shock and awe? What exactly are its dimensions?

Here's my "imaginative guess" regarding the Lord God's throne. *"* *11* The throne is magnificent, somehow radiating out love, joy, and peace. There are beautiful rainbows, lightning, music, and incredible brilliance because God is light. Experiencing God's presence on His throne will be awesome beyond words and treasured by all of us for eternity.

What's your "imaginative guess" for what God's throne will be like? You and I will each be there in this "great multitude" around the very throne of God. We will be thrilled for eternity watching what God will be doing!

? Define

we won't Be just watching

After this, I looked, and there before me was a great multitude that no one could count, from every nation, tribe, people, and language, standing before the throne and before the Lamb. They were wearing white robes and were holding palm branches in their hands. And they cried out in a loud voice: "Salvation belongs to our God, who sits on the throne, and to the Lamb." (Revelation 7:9,10)

There before me was a throne in heaven with someone sitting on it. And the one who sat there had the appearance of jasper and ruby. A rainbow that shone like an emerald encircled the throne. From the throne came flashes of lightning, rumblings, and peals of thunder. Also, in front of the throne, there was what looked like a sea of glass, clear as crystal. (Revelation 4:2-6)

Then I looked and heard the voice of many angels, numbering thousands upon thousands, and ten thousand times ten thousand. They encircled the throne. In a loud voice, they were saying: "Worthy is the Lamb, who was slain, to receive power and wealth and wisdom and strength and honor and glory and praise!" Then I heard every creature in heaven and on earth and under the earth and on the sea, and all that is in them, saying: "To him who sits on the throne and to the Lamb be praise and honor and glory and power, forever and ever!" (Revelation 5:11-13)

Heaven is my throne, and the earth is my footstool. (Isaiah 66:1, Acts 7:49)

The Lord is on his heavenly throne. He observes everyone on earth; his eyes examine them. (Psalm 11:4)

Let us then approach God's throne of grace with confidence so that we may receive mercy and find grace to help us in our time of need. (Hebrews 4:16)

 Notes for reflection

The Trinity Explained

How can we explain the mystery of the Trinity? Many have tried, and I also am going to try! God is one God and exists in three persons who are all God; the Trinity. Our finite minds cannot understand or explain this mystery of God. Here are the basics of what we believe:

- One God and one only
- God exists in three Persons
- All three are equal and eternal
- Each is distinct, yet acting in unity
- The Trinity constitutes the one true God of the Bible

Many Trinitarian analogies have helped to explain the Trinity:

Water: Exists as vapor, liquid, and ice.

Egg: Exists as shell, egg white, and yolk.

Sun: Exists as the sun, which also gives off light and heat.

Creator: Exists as architect, contractor, workman.

Body: (read below).

There are difficulties with each analogy. Here is the Trinitarian analogy that I like the best: God is like a "body." After all, God made us in His image. The Father is the brain who controls and makes the decisions. Jesus is the cardio-pulmonary system (heart, lungs, blood) that gives life. The rest of the body (skin, muscles, digestive system, and all the rest) is the Holy Spirit, who does the work!

There is subordination in the Trinity in that the Father is first, Jesus is His Son, and the Holy Spirit follows to make things happen. Also, the Father sits on the throne in Heaven. Jesus sits to the Father's right. Perhaps the Holy Spirit is in each one of us around the throne.

The Trinity is a mystery that the Bible teaches and should cause us to wonder and worship!

Can you fathom the depths of God or discover the limits of the Almighty? They are higher than the heavens—what can you do? (Job 11:7-8)

As heaven is higher than the earth, so my ways are higher than your ways, and my thoughts than your thoughts. (Isaiah 55:9)

There are many Trinitarian verses:
- Jesus' baptism–(Matthew 3:13-17–the voice of the Father, Son baptized, Spirit is descending like a dove)
- Salvation–(1 Peter 1:2–chosen by the Father, sanctified by the Spirit, sprinkled with the blood of Jesus)
- Sanctification–(2 Corinthians 13:14–the grace of the Lord Jesus, love of God, the fellowship of the Holy Spirit)
- Christian Baptism–(Matthew 28:19–baptized in one name, yet three Persons—Father, Son, and Holy Spirit)
- Prayer–(Ephesians 3:14-21–strengthened by his Spirit, know the love of Christ, filled with the fullness of God)
- Christian Growth–(2 Thessalonians 2:13,14–chosen by God, loved by the Lord, sanctified by the Spirit)

All three persons of the Trinity helped us become followers of Jesus. When we were lost in sin, the Father gave the Son; the Son offered Himself on the Cross, and the Holy Spirit brought us to Jesus; therefore, each member of the Trinity acted to save us.

WE WERE EACH SO LOST THAT IT TOOK EVERY MEMBER OF THE TRINITY TO SAVE US!

Notes for reflection

How is Your Earth Lab Experience Going?

How is your earth "lab experience" going? Did you know that you are the main character in an extraordinary "live laboratory"? Your assignment, and mine, is to be successful for one lifetime. Some will work in the lab for a long time, others a short time. We each have been given a million-dollar body with unique abilities, giftedness, and weaknesses. The Lord has given us His famous "textbook" with directions on how to get an "A" in the lab and pass into eternity successfully.

Unfortunately, Satan has also been allowed into the laboratory to steal, kill, and destroy.

The textbook recommends that we pray to the Lord, seek His direction always, and resist Satan in God's power. Our lab assignment is to love God with everything we have; if there is any energy left over, love our neighbor.

It is exciting to be the main character in this earth lab but also intimidating. Some days it feels as though we are speeding out of control on a roller coaster ride. But don't be anxious. Just put on your spiritual seat belt and settle back to enjoy your incredible "earth lab." Your textbook will give you the best instructions. You will be amazed at the experience! Look forward to your "A+."

Too Clever

Peace I leave with you; my peace I give you. I do not give to you as the world gives. Do not let your hearts be troubled and do not be afraid. (John 14:27)

But seek first the kingdom of God and His righteousness, and all these things will be added to you. (Matthew 6:31-33)

Now may God equip you with everything good that you may do His will, working in us that which is pleasing in His sight through Jesus Christ. (Hebrews 13:20,21)

So we can confidently say, "The Lord is my helper; I will not fear." (Hebrews 13:6)

"For I know the plans I have for you," declares the Lord, "plans to prosper you and not to harm you, plans to give you hope and a future." (Jeremiah 29:11)

Therefore, submit to God. Resist the devil, and he will flee from you. Draw near to God, and He will draw near to you. (James 4:7-8)

These things I have spoken to you, that my joy may be in you and that your joy may be full. (John 15:11)

Jesus replied: "Love the Lord your God with all your heart and with all your soul and with all your mind." (Luke 10:27, Mark 12:30, Matthew 22:37)

Well done, good and faithful servant! You have been faithful with a few things; I will put you in charge of many things. (Luke 19:17, Matthew 25:21)

 Notes for reflection

There are Well-Worn Trails

See

There are well-worn trails to walk along for each of us to achieve spiritual maturity. The three most common routes are "fellowship," "Bible study," and "prayer." But how can we make these three activities more exciting than TV, screen time, and all the other fun things life has to offer?

While that may seem impossible, what we know is that spiritual activities become more and more exciting as you move down the three trails. Often people receive supernatural "God-sightings" to help on the way. That's really exciting! The Lord encourages each person with a sense of personal relationship and closeness to Him that is hard to express in words. Often when walking with God, you will experience a "high" which provides you with a fantastic experience not possible by watching TV or screens.

While the three paths to spiritual maturity are well known, Satan can trick a person into confusing, dangerous side trails. It's easy to see the hazardous ways others are walking, but challenging to see our own perilous path. Pray that the Lord will keep you from stumbling down the wrong trail.

A word of caution is in order. Try to avoid tempting "pity party" paths and enticing "gossipy" trails. Anger bushes and inappropriate "playgrounds" are off-limits. Also, be wary of "despair/worry" swamps in your way. Look to Jesus and His friends to help you out.

How is your trail working for you this week? Perhaps you could ask another "Jesus sojourner" to walk alongside and enjoy the journey with you?

Therefore, as you received Christ Jesus the Lord, so walk in him, rooted and built up in him and established in the faith, just as you were taught, abounding in thanksgiving. (Colossians 2:6,7)

"For I know the plans I have for you," declares the Lord, "plans to prosper you and not to harm you, plans to give you hope and a future. Then you will call on me and come and pray to me, and I will listen to you. You will seek me and find me when you seek me with all your heart. I will be found by you," declares the Lord. (Jeremiah 29:11-14)

I am certain that God, who began the good work within you, will continue his work until it is finally finished on the day when Christ Jesus returns. (Philippians 1:6)

Whoever has my commands and keeps them is the one who loves me. The one who loves me will be loved by my Father, and I too will love them and show myself to them. (John 14:21)

But you will receive power when the Holy Spirit comes on you, and you will be my witnesses in Jerusalem, and in all Judea and Samaria, and to the ends of the earth. (Acts 1:8)

 **Notes for reflection**

How Long is Eternity?

Eternity is beyond our comprehension. Eternity is infinite, with no end on either side. The more we think about the "ends" of eternity, the bigger the middle becomes. But, we can't comprehend the ends of eternity because there are no ends!

Therefore, let me simply try to enlarge the middle between the ends of eternity. "Amazing Grace" last verse: "When we've been there 10,000 years...We've no less days to sing God's praise then when we've first begun." That's our starting place. After 10,000 years, we will have experienced just the first little bit of eternity.

Woody Allen quipped that "eternity is very long, especially towards the end." That sarcasm helps us grapple with eternity a bit more. How does the following example of eternity work for you? Imagine an eagle every 100 years, placing one grain of sand out on a big flat area. When that pile of sand finally reaches the height of Mount Everest (the highest mountain in the world), eternity has just begun.

That's about as good as I can do trying to describe how long eternity is. What's even more astounding is trying to imagine ourselves in eternity. You and I will be alive for eternity! We did indeed have a beginning "start time," but we will not have an "end time." This "earth lab" is crucial for each of us because it determines where we will be for eternity. Jp

God, who is in control of eternity, has created us specifically to spend eternity enjoying Him and His love. While we can't fully understand eternity, we can experience His love at present. For now, anticipate eternity where we will be discovering more and more of God's love forever and ever and ever!

We know and rely on the love God has for us. God is love. (1 John 4:16)

My sheep listen to my voice; I know them, and they follow me. I give them eternal life, and they shall never perish. (John 10:27,28)

For we know that if the earthly tent we live in is destroyed, we have a building from God, an eternal house in heaven, not built by human hands. (2 Corinthians 5:1)

My Father's house has many rooms, and I go and prepare a place for you. I will come back and take you to be with me that you may be where I am. (John 14:2,3)

What no eye has seen, what no ear has heard, and what no human mind has conceived—the things God has prepared for those who love him. (1 Corinthians 2:9)

What good is it for someone to gain the whole world and yet lose or forfeit their very self? (Luke 9:25)

You make known to me the path of life; you will fill me with joy in your presence, with eternal pleasures at your right hand. (Psalm 16:11)

 **Notes for reflection**

The Gift of Poverty

The "Gift of Poverty" sounds like a pretty lousy gift. How can poverty be a gift? We all struggle to keep from being poor and living in poverty. If you keep finding your funds to be limited, consider what a Godly "gift" poverty might be!

First off, know that Heaven will be occupied primarily by poor people. These "poor" people greatly depend on God for rain and food and a place to stay. The "gift of poverty" has caused them to pray hard and trust in God, and they have found that He is faithful. *[handwritten: Speculation — Not Always]*

Wealth is dangerous if it allows people to "trust" in their wealth instead of trusting God's provision. Wealth might be one of Satan's most potent tools to entice people away from God. What is "your price" for Satan to steal you from Jesus?

One of A. W. Tozer's vows for spiritual power is this: "Own nothing; everything you own is God's, and He has lovingly borrowed it to you." Remember, if you are a millionaire, that your money belongs to God. Count your many blessings but know that God has borrowed the money to you for His glory!

In conclusion, we are all wealthy compared to most in the world. Be very, very grateful for each penny and realize it's God's money entrusted to you for His glory. That doesn't mean that you need to give all your money away and become a poor person. Use the money He has entrusted you with to receive real joy, thrill, and eternal happiness! Pray, and He will show you how to use it wisely.

[handwritten: What do you mean?]

Yet true godliness with contentment is itself great wealth. (1 Timothy 6:6)

Honor the Lord with your wealth and with the best part of everything you produce. (Proverbs 3:9)

It is easier for a camel to go through the eye of a needle than for a rich person to enter the Kingdom of God! (Matthew 19:24)

Give me neither poverty nor riches! Give me just enough to satisfy my needs. (Proverbs 30:8)

Though our Lord Jesus Christ was rich, yet for your sakes, he became poor, so that by his poverty he could make you rich. (2 Corinthians 8:9)

Don't store up treasures here on earth where thieves break in and steal. Store your treasures in heaven. Wherever your treasure is, there your heart will be also. (Matthew 6:19-21)

He gave five bags of silver to one, two bags of silver to another, and one bag of silver to the last—dividing it in proportion to their abilities. He then left on his trip. When the master returned, he was full of praise. "Well done, my good and faithful servant. You have been faithful in handling these five bags, so now I will give you many more responsibilities." (Matthew 25:19-21)

I know about your suffering and your poverty—but you are rich! (Revelation 2:9)

Keep your life free from love of money, and be content with what you have. (Hebrews 13:5-6)

 Notes for reflection

We are Sharing the Holy Spirit with Many Others

We are sharing the Holy Spirit with over one and a half billion people today. Seven and one-half billion people are alive in the world; about one-fourth of them are Christians. Therefore, we are sharing the Holy Spirit with many other people today. Does He have any energy left to help you and me? Could He be on overload, putting His power and resources into others more important than you and I?

How can the Holy Spirit do everything with each of us? That answer is simple; the Holy Spirit is God. He has all power; He knows, everything and has all wisdom. It is simple for Him to be in each of us, doing everything that needs to be done. There is no problem; He is accomplishing it perfectly! *? WHAT'S IT ?*

When we become followers of Jesus, the Holy Spirit enters into us, and we become new creatures. It is excellent news that the Holy Spirit is our teacher and helper. He is also our deposit and guarantee that each of us will go to heaven. We seriously need Him in us! *Alien people*

It's simple for Him to counsel and empower each one of us. Rejoice greatly in your perfect "teacher," "helper," "counselor," "deposit," and "guarantee." Give thanks that He is doing a great job with you!

christianese

common mind would not follow with this meaning !

Therefore, if anyone is in Christ, the new creation has come: The old has gone, the new is here! (2 Corinthians 5:17)

And I will ask the Father, and he will give you the Holy Spirit to help you and be with you forever, for he lives in you. (John 14:16,17)

When you believed, you were marked in him with a seal, the promised Holy Spirit, who is a deposit guaranteeing our inheritance. (Ephesians 1:13,14)

But the Advocate, the Holy Spirit, will teach you all things and will remind you of everything I have said to you. (John 14:26)

In the same way, the Spirit helps us in our weakness. We do not know what we ought to pray for, but the Spirit himself intercedes for us through wordless groans. The Spirit intercedes for God's people in accordance with the will of God. (Romans 8:26,27)

 Notes for reflection

Your Valuable "Deposit" to Get into Heaven

The Holy Spirit is your deposit, guaranteeing that you will get into heaven. He's your "down payment," so to speak, and might be your most valuable possession. Your "down payment" deposit didn't cost you anything. A sizeable down payment is usually needed to buy a house. Not so for you to get into heaven; all you need is your Holy Spirit deposit.

To get your deposit, ask Jesus to "forgive your sin" and be "Lord of your life." With that simple request, you have invited the Holy Spirit to come into your life forever. Isn't that amazing? What a deal! That is the best deal on planet earth!

DEAL w/ DEVIL ?

Not only is the Holy Spirit your guarantee for heaven, but He also guides, comforts, gives advice, heals, and the list of benefits goes on and on. Most importantly, the Holy Spirit is closer than your closest friend; He will help you in more ways than you can imagine. Ask Him to help you love the Father and Jesus with all your heart, mind, and strength. Then wait and see what happens!

WITH GOD ?

MOST PEOPLE ASSOCIATE WITH EMPLOYMENT

When you believed, you were marked in him with a seal, the promised Holy Spirit, who is a deposit guaranteeing our inheritance until the redemption of those who are God's possession—to the praise of his glory. (Ephesians 1:13,14)

Do you not know that your bodies are temples of the Holy Spirit, who is in you, whom you have received from God? (1 Corinthians 6:19)

The Holy Spirit gives, to believers, spiritual fruit such as "love, joy, peace" (Galatians 5:22) and spiritual gifts: "healing, preaching, evangelism." (1 Corinthians 12:7-11)

We do not know what we ought to pray for, but the Spirit himself intercedes for us through wordless groans. (Romans 8:26)

But you will receive power when the Holy Spirit comes on you, and you will be my witnesses in Jerusalem and to the ends of the earth. (Acts 1:8)

 Notes for reflection

Is God's Power Available to Us?

How much of God's power is available to us? Maybe we shouldn't know; we might become proud or dangerous to ourselves and others. Guard yourselves with profound humility as we consider how much of God's power we can unleash! — MAKE IT SOUND LIKE

Paul prays that we will understand this power available to us. He SUPER HERO AVENGERS! describes three levels of power in these verses:

"I pray that the eyes of your heart may be enlightened in order that you may know...his incomparably great power for us who believe. That power is (#1) the same as the mighty strength he exerted when he raised Christ from the dead and (#2) seated him at his right hand in the heavenly realms, far above all rule and authority, power and dominion, and every name that is invoked, (#3) not only in the present age but also in the one to come". (Ephesians 1:18-21)

Those three levels of power available to us are incredible!

Level #1. The power to raise Christ from the dead after three days of death with cell deterioration is supernatural. Only God has that much power. How can that much power be available to us?

Level #2. The power to take Jesus from the earth and seat Him in heaven above all others takes incredible supernatural power!

Level #3. The supernatural power to live forever in eternity, not just for a few years but for eternity!

How can we humans have that much power available to cause #1, #2, and #3 to occur? Paul prays that each of us will understand that, in Christ, we have that much power! Can you believe it? Here is one power challenge that you might try:

Pray for someone you love to become a follower of Jesus: a Christian. When God answers your prayer, that person will be raised from the dead (#1), seated with Christ in the Heavenly realms (#2), and live forever (#3)!

Your prayers are powerful!

IF

WHAT WILL THEY DO WHEN THEY TRY & PERSON DOESN'T BECOME A CHRISTIAN

NOW? LATER?

NO MEANING TO MOST PEOPLE / NOW? LATER?

39

The prayer of a righteous person is powerful and effective. (James 5:16)

And I will do whatever you ask in my name, so that the Father may be glorified in the Son. You may ask me for anything in my name, and I will do it. (John 14:13,14)

And God raised us up with Christ and seated us with him in the heavenly realms in Christ Jesus. (Ephesians 2:6)

Surely your goodness and mercy will follow me all the days of my life, and I will dwell in the house of the Lord forever. (Psalm 23:6)

 Notes for reflection

Does God Need Us?

Do you think that God needs us? God is entirely sufficient. He is not dependent on us and would do perfectly well without us. Would God be less if we didn't exist? "No." Would God be more if we are alive? "No." God is entirely sufficient without us.

On the other hand, God has each hair on our head numbered! That seems like a significant effort and speaks loudly regarding His care for detail in our lives. Furthermore, He made each of us for a particular purpose according to this verse: "For we are God's handiwork, created in Christ Jesus to do good works, which God prepared in advance for us to do." (Ephesians 2:10)

There is so much proof that God, the Father, and Jesus, must love us very deeply. God loved us so much that He sent Jesus to die in our place so that we could live with Him forever. God doesn't need us, but He does love us. If God loves us, He must need us!

Many things are a mystery; God, who doesn't need us, chose to need us. That would seem to be a loving but daring decision. So let us humbly respond by choosing to "love the Lord with all our heart, mind, soul, and strength." Don't be like the "runaway bride" and miss out on the thrilling purpose for which He created you!

For God so loved the world, that he gave his only Son, that whoever believes in him should not perish but have eternal life. (John 3:16)

But God demonstrates his love for us in this: While we were still sinners, Christ died for us. (Romans 5:8)

And even the very hairs of your head are all numbered. (Matthew 10:30)

Surely your goodness and mercy will follow me all the days of my life, and I will dwell in the house of the Lord forever. (Psalm 23:6)

Let us rejoice and be glad and give him glory! For the wedding of the Lamb has come, and his bride has made herself ready. (Revelation 19:7)

For we know how dearly God loves us because he has given us the Holy Spirit to fill our hearts with his love. (Romans 5:5)

You are a chosen people. You are royal priests, a holy nation, God's very own possession. (1 Peter 2:9)

Notes for reflection

How Small and How Big Can God Make Things?

How small can God create something? He made the "quark." Perhaps that is the smallest thing until scientists find something smaller. A quark is .00000000000000001 meter (or $10^{-18.2}$). What is the biggest thing that God can make? Would it be the universe? The universe is currently 156 billion light-years from end to end (or 5.5×10^{23} miles in length). A light-year is the distance light travels in one year and is 5.9 trillion miles. Also, scientists believe the universe is expanding at an incredible speed in all directions.

The Bible states that "In the beginning, God created the heavens and the earth." Some scientists who struggle with belief in God are trying desperately to postulate another cause of creation. It is not that scientists are wrong in their creation theories; they are wrong to theorize that God did not make it happen as they theorize.

Scientists claim that everything started with a big bang 13.8 billion years ago from something the size of a hydrogen atom. Who made that hydrogen atom? That said, they are getting closer to the Biblical truth that God created the heavens and the earth. The Bible says, "out of nothing." *WHO MADE THAT SOMETHING*

God makes things very small, and He makes things very big! Now picture God holding the entire expanding universe in His hand as though He were holding a basketball. What you have just visualized is one reason why "Lord God Almighty" is mentioned 93 times in the Bible. He is the God we worship!

In the beginning, God created the heavens and the earth. (Genesis 1:1)

Ah, Sovereign Lord, you have made the heavens and the earth by your great power and outstretched arm. Nothing is too hard for you. (Jeremiah 32:17)

Every house is built by someone, but God is the builder of every-thing. (Hebrews 3:4)

For since the creation of the world, God's invisible qualities—his eternal power and divine nature—have been clearly seen, being understood from what has been made, so that people are without excuse. (Romans 1:20)

By the word of the Lord, the heavens were made, their starry host by the breath of his mouth. Our help is in the name of the Lord, the Maker of heaven and earth. (Psalm 33:6, 124:8)

Do you not know? Have you not heard? The Lord is the everlasting God, the Creator of the ends of the earth. He will not grow tired or weary, and his understanding no one can fathom. (Isaiah 40:28)

 Notes for reflection

Faith as Small as a Mustard Seed

What's the least amount of faith needed to get into heaven? That's easy! Only a tiny amount is required. The Bible says that faith as small as a mustard seed will allow nothing to be impossible for you. Just a small size is enough faith to #1 – Ask Jesus to forgive your sins, and #2 – Know that Jesus rose from the dead, and #3 – Ask Him to be Lord of your life. *? WHAT IS THAT ?*

Some people think that becoming a Christian is such a complicated process. Actually, following Jesus is pretty straightforward. You don't even need to know answers to difficult spiritual questions. Becoming a Christian is easy, and such a "no brainer." The rewards *? Spell out* are great. We can have a blessed life now and eternal life in the future. Heaven is free; it is terrific. Don't let anything rob you of its unimaginable riches. The penalties for not acting in faith are significant. The Bible describes hell as pain, total darkness, and isolation. Step up in the faith! GO TO HEAVEN! *Christianese*

Accepting Jesus as Savior and Lord can all happen gloriously in one last gasp of life, but don't wait until then. You will lose out on so much "abundant life"! (John 10:10b)

Know what your saying but its not true!

Truly I tell you, if you have faith as small as a mustard seed, you can say to this mountain, "Move from here to there," and it will move. Nothing will be impossible for you. (Matthew 17:20)

If you confess with your mouth that "Jesus is Lord" and believe in your heart that God raised him from the dead, you will be saved. (Romans 10:9,10)

Believe in the Lord Jesus, and you will be saved—you and your household. (Acts 16:31)

Then the thief on the cross said, "Jesus, remember me when you come into your kingdom." Jesus answered him, "Truly, I tell you, today you will be with me in paradise." (Luke 23:42,43)

For heaven's sake," but more importantly, for your own sake, get into heaven!

 **Notes for reflection**

IS THAT THE GOAL ?
THE MOTIVATION
CHRIST'S WORK
THRU LOVE —
GOAL IS
OBEDIENCE

On my own "FAITH STAIRCASE"!

[handwritten: Competition or Scale of Merit?]

We are each on our own private ("faith staircase.") It is a very tall staircase, and each of us is partially up and partially down it. The greater your faith in God and His promises, the higher the step on which you are standing. The bottom step is for those with lesser faith who have just begun to follow Jesus. Most people desire to go higher on the stairs because one's view of life starts to clear, and it is much more exciting the more they go up! *[handwritten: Not true]*

It's not lonely on the staircase. You can see others on their stairs and talk with them if you desire. If a severe difficulty comes your way, don't fall off your faith staircase! Just hold on tightly to Jesus; He will keep you from falling. *[handwritten: ?]*

How did you get as far up as you are on your staircase? Did you have Godly parents or excellent friends, or a church group? There are many good ways to help you go higher on your staircase. Here are some quick suggestions: *[handwritten: NO]*

1. Pray daily for more faith—This prayer is a bit dangerous because the Lord may send difficulties to increase your faith.
2. Read the Bible. Faith increases by hearing the Word.
3. Find a friend or two who have more faith than you have and try to catch up with them. *[handwritten: ? NO!!!! - NOT BIBLICAL]*
4. Enjoy church and be with other friends there. *[handwritten: Run your RACE!]*
5. Share your faith with someone lower on their staircase who has less faith than yourself.

[handwritten: ? o]
[handwritten: How do you know?]
[handwritten: NOT A STAIRWAY JOURNEY maybe STORY - for sure]

Without faith, it's impossible to please God because anyone who comes to Him must believe that he exists and that he rewards those who earnestly seek him. (Hebrews 11:6)

Faith comes from hearing and hearing through the word of Christ. (Romans 10:17)

If you have faith as small as a mustard seed, you can say to this mountain, "Move from here to there," and it will move. Nothing will be impossible for you. (Matthew 17:20)

Fix your eyes on Jesus, the pioneer and perfecter of our faith. (Hebrews 12:2)

For it is by grace you have been saved through faith, and this is not from yourselves, it is the gift of God—not by works, so that no one can boast. (Ephesians 2:8,9)

There are faith, hope, and love; the greatest of these is love. (1 Corinthians 13:13 - but faith must be pretty great also!)

 Notes for reflection

Pray "the Dangerous Prayer"!

Pray "the dangerous prayer":

"I love you, Father. Help me to love you more!"

"I love you, Jesus. Help me to love you more!"

"I love you, Holy Spirit. Help me to love you more!"

Okay, it's really six small prayers. If you feel brave, pray that dangerous prayer once and see what happens. If nothing happens differently from usual, pray it again. If nothing happens, pray it again; stop praying it after about a thousand times!

So what is so dangerous about these prayers? It is scary to re-alize that God may need to do something to get our attention. What does God have to do for you to love Him more? If you are afraid to pray these prayers, you can add on a disclaimer, "Lord, help me love you more but please without pain!" That's okay, but it may limit God in helping you to love Him to the max. Still, it's okay.

Pray dangerously each day; then, wait expectantly for "God sight-ings" in your life. God will answer your prayers. Keep your spiritual eyes open for "divine appointments" and increased intimacy with the Lord that you will experience!

And you must love the Lord your God with all your heart, all your soul, and all your strength. (Deuteronomy 6:5, Mark 12:30, Luke 10:27, Matthew 22:37 Wow – God must mean it!)

Be strong and courageous. Do not be afraid; do not be discouraged, for the Lord your God will be with you wherever you go. (Joshua 1:9)

Ask, and you will receive. (Matthew 7:7)

You may ask me for anything in my name, and I will do it. (John 14:14)

Daily Maintenance Prayers

WHAT ARE you ASKING? — Jayish?

Daily maintenance prayers may seem a bit boring. They are a bit like brushing your teeth or doing dishes every day. What's with those maintenance prayers? How powerful are they?

I generally don't put a lot of energy into them; I just pray them regularly. They are the prayers for the family, our health, jobs, etc. They're just maintenance prayers; we pray them over and over again. Are they powerful? Here is an answer:

God's power behind those routine prayers might not seem to be so much each day; however, each prayer stacks God's power a little higher when you pray it. Daily praying turns them into an incredible force. Daily prayers grow taller and taller, and eventually, they are like massive towers that change the future skyline forever!

Even after we die, those massive prayer towers will continue exerting God's power day after day. Your daily maintenance prayers may even grow up into huge skyscrapers. Know that the Lord will powerfully use your maintenance prayers. Don't stop!

? WHAT ?

Pray continually. (1Thessalonians 5:17)

Jesus told them. "I tell you the truth, if you had faith even as small as a mustard seed, you could say to this mountain, 'Move from here to there,' and it would move. Nothing would be impossible." (Matthew 17:20)

This is how you should pray: Our Father in heaven, hallowed be your name. (Matthew 6:9)

So Jesus left them and went away once more and prayed the third time, saying the same thing. (Matthew 26:44)

In the same way, the Spirit helps us in our weakness. We do not know what we ought to pray for, but the Spirit himself intercedes for us through wordless groans. (Romans 8:26)

Then Jesus told his disciples a parable to show them that they should always pray and not give up. (Luke 18:1)

 **Notes for reflection**

Pray for your Grandchildren

What happens when you pray for your grandchildren to know the Lord? What happens with that prayer, and how can you make it more powerful?

Here are some possibilities:

1. Pray twice so that your prayer has double the impact. If you feel your prayer is weak, then pray ten times or more. Do whatever it takes!

2. Pray using the Scripture below.

3. Cleanse yourself personally. Get rid of sin by asking for forgiveness and be right with God as much as possible.

4. Fasting hurts, but attempt to fast a time or two for your prayer's effectiveness. You might do well to let your grandchildren know you fasted as well. It can't hurt.

5. Every prayer you pray exerts spiritual energy to accomplish God's saving power with your grandchild. Every prayer pushes him/her a bit closer toward getting right with God. Envision the Lord's spiritual energy touching your loved one every time you pray.

6. Push your grandchildren spiritually. It may destroy your relationship with them, but they should know that a life without the Lord is not okay with you or God. You might mention to your grandchild that God is very powerful and can easily answer their prayers if they pray.

7. Realize that your fervent prayers will continue powerfully, affecting your grandchildren after you die. Don't become discouraged. A little faith will move a mountain, and your grandchild is small compared to any mountain.

Ask anything in my Name, and I will do it that the Father might be glorified. (John 14:14)

I tell you the truth, if you had faith even as small as a mustard seed, you could say to this mountain, "Move from here to there," and it would move. Nothing would be impossible. (Matthew 17:20)

The prayer of a righteous person is powerful and effective. (James 5:16)

 Notes for reflection

Is It Possible to Pray "Afterwards"?

Is it possible to pray for something that has already passed in time? Imagine that you promised to pray for your friend's surgery, but you forgot. The surgery has finished, and you haven't prayed. Can you pray for the surgery even after it has ended?

Your first thought is, "why even try"? Since it has already happened, how could prayer change anything? WHOA! God is "timeless," and He is in the past, present, and the future. Even before the surgery started, God knew that you would be praying for His blessing on the surgery. He has already answered the prayer He knew you would pray!

When you hear of a friend or loved one who has died, ask God to have given that person the desire to ask Jesus for salvation before their death. Your prayer might make the difference between eternal life and death for your friend.

From His eternal perspective outside of time, God knows everything whether in the past, the present, or the future. By now, is your head spinning and a bit confused about all this? It's okay. We don't need to understand; we just need to keep on praying! That's the important thing.

Your Father knows what you need before you ask him. (Matthew 6:8)

Before they call, I will answer; while they are yet speaking, I will hear. (Isaiah 65:24)

I am the Alpha and the Omega, says the Lord God, who is, and who was, and who is to come, the Almighty. (Revelation 1:8)

If you have faith as small as a mustard seed, nothing will be impossible for you. (Matthew 17:20)

What Happens in Heaven when you say: "I Love You Jesus"

What happens in heaven when you say, "I love you Jesus"? It is such a quick, easy prayer. We tend to think it flies up to Jesus, who hears it, smiles, and winks down at us. Then "poof"; it is all gone. If that's what happens, that's great. We should probably say it more often, don't you think?

It's just possible, however, that "I love you" accomplishes far more! We will find out when we enter into eternity, but for now, imagine that this is what happens. "I love you Jesus" enters heaven and goes directly to God's throne room where the Father, Son, and Holy Spirit are enjoying "love" from earthlings.

Because of that one simple "love" prayer, a superb lightning show begins. Somehow the words: "I love you Jesus" expand into amazing music with trumpets and drums. Thousands of angels are thrilled by the love message from just one Christian praying down here on earth.

Furthermore, if there is passion or tears behind the "I love you," the music's intensity is expanded, and the length of incredible grandeur quadruples. Passionate prayers on earth may provide a magnificent heavenly show beyond our imagination! Want some verses to help you envision it?

Now to him who is able to do immeasurably more than all we ask or imagine, according to His power that is at work within us. (Ephesians 3:20)

There before me was a throne in heaven; a rainbow that shone like an emerald encircled the throne. From the throne came flashes of lightning, rumblings, and peals of thunder. Also, in front of the throne, there was what looked like a sea of glass, clear as crystal. Holy, holy, holy is the Lord God Almighty, who was, and is, and is to come. (Revelation 4:2-11)

Then I heard what sounded like a great multitude, like the roar of rushing waters and like loud peals of thunder, shouting, "Hallelujah! For our Lord God Almighty reigns." (Revelation 19:6)

Jesus replied: "Love the Lord your God with all your heart and with all your soul and with all your mind." (Matthew 22:37)

P.S. There is a special bonus for those who pray that prayer: get ready for Jesus to reveal Himself to you. "The one who loves me will be loved by my Father, and I too will love them and show myself to them." (John 14:21)

 Notes for reflection

Lord, Help Me to Love You More

Lord, help me to "love you more." We know the greatest command-ment: "Love the Lord your God with all your heart and with all your soul and with all your mind and with all your strength." (Mark 12:30) How can we love God more? Sometimes it is helpful to look at the four things we are to love the Lord with:

#1 Heart (emotions)

#2 Soul (inner being or spiritual part of you)

#3 Mind (intellect)

#4 Strength (energy)

Here are some possible ideas to increase each of those areas of your "God love."

#1 Heart/emotions – Consider listening to emotional Christian songs, movies, books, and testimonies.

#2 Soul/spiritual – Deal ruthlessly with sin, surrender every-thing you have to God. He will borrow back to you whatever you need. Give spiritual disciplines your best effort.

#3 Mind/intellect – Seek Bible knowledge with Bible study, memorization, sermons, books, and much more.

#4 Strength/energy – Be tired at the end of the day doing #1 to #3 plus good works to love your neighbor.

Did you notice the four "alls" in the Great Commandment? That is exhausting and impossible! How can we give one hundred percent of ourselves to each of those four areas? Praise the Lord for His compassion and mercy to us.

We love him (God) because he first loved us. (1 John 4:19 KJV)

The Lord, the Lord, the compassionate and gracious God, slow to anger, abounding in love and faithfulness, maintaining love to thou-sands, and forgiving wickedness, rebellion, and sin. (Exodus 34:6,7)

The Lord is full of compassion and mercy. (James 5:11)

Therefore, I urge you, brothers and sisters, in view of God's mercy, to offer your bodies as a living sacrifice, holy and pleasing to God—this is your true and proper worship. (Romans 12:1)

 Notes for reflection

The Trapdoor

Have you heard about the hidden "trapdoor" at the foot of the Cross? What follows is a quick explanation of this elusive trapdoor. The scenario starts when a mature Christian goes to the Cross, where Jesus died, and leaves his heavy burden there.

Here's the problem. After dropping the burden at the Cross, a person might quickly pick it up again. How about you? How much time passes before you pick up at least part of the heavy burden and limp away groaning because of the weight?

Here is good news. There is a figurative trap door at the foot of the Cross. It's a bit hidden in the grass, but it's there. This trap door, if lifted, covers a deep hole from which nothing returns. You put something in there, and it's gone, gone, gone! No matter how hard you try, you will never be able to reach it and put it on your back. It's gone completely. Say, "goodbye, yucky burden, forever!"

Spiritually, you need to find that trapdoor next time you want to get rid of your burden. It is somewhere there at the foot of the Cross, and you can find it if you seek it. Take your load, open the trapdoor, and throw it down.

Try dumping something small at first just for practice. Once you get the hang of it spiritually, dump some more significant burdens down the trapdoor. If you wonder where it went, imagine a big fire in which Jesus incinerates stuff like that. Celebrate it being gone with a great sigh of thanksgiving.

As you become a garbage dumper for the Lord, tell your best friend about your discovery. He or she might need the trapdoor even more than you do.

Cast your burden upon the Lord, and He will sustain you; He will never allow the righteous to be shaken. (Psalm 55:22)

Come to me, all you who are weary and burdened, and I will give you rest. (Matthew 11;28)

As far as the east is from the west, so far has he removed our transgressions from us. (Psalm 103:12)

If we confess our sins, he is faithful and just and will forgive us our sins and purify us from all unrighteousness. (1 John 1:9)

Do not be anxious about anything, but in every situation, by prayer and petition, with thanksgiving, present your requests to God. And the peace of God, which transcends all understanding, will guard your hearts and your minds in Christ Jesus. (Philippians 4:6,7)

And I will do whatever you ask in my name, so that the Father may be glorified in the Son. You may ask me for anything in my name, and I will do it. (John 14:13,14)

 Notes for reflection

Glorious Yummy Food

Aren't you amazed by glorious, yummy food?

Plants eat dirt - yummy, yummy dirt.

Cars eat gasoline - yummy, yummy gas.

Computers eat electricity - yummy, yummy electrons.

We humans eat yummy food. Refreshing, tasty, luscious, satisfying, chewy, crunchy, fantastic food. What a great idea the Lord had to let us eat excellent food instead of dirt, gasoline, or electricity. Food is so fun, so exciting, so tasty!

It could have been so different and not nearly as much fun. Food is proof that God loves each of us so much! He gave us great appetites for glorious food three times a day plus snacks almost whenever we want. Chocolate always works pretty well; prime rib and buttered potatoes, soda, and chips; the list goes on.

But here is what I think the Lord may be teaching us. If your appetites in life miss out on God, you miss out on that which satisfies our needs and cravings the most. "Eat of the Lord" and taste and see that He is the most satisfying.

Taste and see that the Lord is good; blessed is the one who takes refuge in him. (Psalm 34:8)

Take and eat; this is my body. Then he took a cup, and when he had given thanks, he gave it to them, saying, drink from it. This is my blood of the covenant, which is poured out for many for the forgiveness of sins. (Matthew 26:26-28)

Like newborn babies, crave pure spiritual milk so that by it you may grow up in your salvation, now that you have tasted that the Lord is good. (1 Peter 2:2,3)

How sweet are your words to my taste, sweeter than honey to my mouth! (Psalm 119:103)

Jesus answered and said to her, "Whoever drinks of this water will thirst again, but whoever drinks of the water that I shall give him will never thirst. The water that I shall give him will become in him a fountain of water springing up into everlasting life." (John 4:13,14)

 Notes for reflection

Forgiveness and Poop

"If we confess our sins, God is faithful and will forgive our sins and cleanse us from all unrighteousness." The relationship between 1 John 1:9 and poop is so simple, so self-explanatory. Why even write about it? On the other hand, hardly anyone has ever thought about the relationship between this verse and bathrooms. Let's think about it, but only briefly.

Sin is very much like stool or poop or "waste." Our bodies need to get rid of the waste, or we get distended and die. In like manner, we followers of Jesus need to get rid of our sin, or die with sin and not get into Heaven. *BAD PHRASE* *poor THeology*

Jesus died on the Cross to take our sin away. It doesn't occur automatically, though; we each need to confess and ask Jesus to take it, or it doesn't happen. It's so simple to ask Jesus to flush our sins away. That's where 1 John 1:9 comes in: "If we confess our sins, he is faithful and just and will forgive us our sins and purify us from all unrighteousness."

No one likes poop. On the other hand, many people seem to like sin; some actually brag about their sin. They flaunt it and want others to enjoy sin also. They would never do that with their poop. Let me give some examples of people wearing poop.

Some people swear using God's name in an unholy way. That is like smearing waste on themselves; it just doesn't look attractive. The Ten Commandments help define some other nasty poop like stealing, lying, and more.

There are many folks, however, who would like to get rid of all waste. It's easy to do; get rid of it! Confess it and ask Jesus to take that sin away.

WHole pAge JusT wonders TO use wowr poop?

63

The Ten Commandments. (Exodus 20, Deuteronomy 5)

1 Have no other gods before me.

2 Don't worship idols.

3 Don't misuse the name of God.

4 Keep the Sabbath day holy.

5 Respect your father and mother.

6 Don't kill others.

7 Don't have sex with someone's spouse.

8 Don't steal.

9 Don't lie.

10 Don't covet your neighbor's wife or property.

 Notes for reflection

The Scariest Place

Where is the scariest place in all of creation? As a kid, it was under my bed when the lights were out. Later Halloween scare parks and horror movies terrified me momentarily. Now, to be in a terrible car accident or, worse yet, being burned alive at the stake would top the list.

The Bible is very expressive about the scariest place. Jesus talked about that place more than He spoke of heaven. Because it is so frightening, people should be scared of going there. There is eternal fire, isolation forever, and lots of pain. We don't even want to think about hell.

Hell is the culmination of folks telling God to "go away." After persistently telling that message to God, He finally says, "have your way." So that's how people choose to go to that scary place. They will find the road to go there is wide and easy to follow.

On the other hand, if we quit "stiff-arming" God and turn to Jesus, we choose eternity without fire and pain. Follow Jesus and hold on tightly to experience your "ultimate adventure." You will be thrilled for eternity!

The thief comes only to steal and kill and destroy; I have come that they may have life and have it to the full. (John 10:10)

Enter by the narrow gate, for the gate that leads to destruction is wide and easy and those who enter by it are many. (Matthew 7:13-14)

And if anyone's name was not found written in the book of life, he was thrown into the lake of fire. (Revelation 20:15)

Then he will say to those on his left, "Depart from me, you who are cursed, into the eternal fire prepared for the devil and his angels. And these will go away into eternal punishment, but the righteous into eternal life." (Matthew 25:41,46)

If you declare with your mouth, "Jesus is Lord" and believe in your heart that God raised him from the dead, you will be saved. (Romans 10:9)

 Notes for reflection

Open Your "Spiritual Eyes"

Where is the most beautiful, incredible place in all of God's creation? There are so many magnificent places to choose from: an ocean beach or a mountain peak. In addition to what we usually think of, there may be microscopic beauty beyond our comprehension, beauty under the sea, and magnificent sights far away in other galaxies.

To make this beautiful place even more spectacular, add in the perfect temperature with a nice breeze and no mosquitoes, please. Now it's becoming a fabulous place! Is there food nearby? Where is that place, and let's go! Wait a minute, though; somehow, I think we've missed the very best, excellent location. Any ideas?

Without question, the most incredible place in all creation will be right where God is! To be able to see God and His glory will be breathtaking! Also, the closer we get to God, the more incredible it will be. The love, joy, and thrill will increase with each step closer we take. Although we can hardly imagine what it will be like, a meaningful exercise might be to envision it with our "spiritual eyes."

Heaven will be a terrific adventure of supernatural experiences. In your prayer time today, see how close you can get to God! Shut your eyes, then open up your "spiritual eyes" to feel the love coming to you from the Father. Now walk closer towards that love!

You will fill me with joy in your presence, with eternal pleasures at your right hand. (Psalm 16:11)

No eye has seen, nor ear heard, nor the heart of man imagined, what God has prepared for those who love him. (1 Corinthians 2:9)

And God raised us up with Christ and seated us with him in the heavenly realms in Christ Jesus, in order that in the coming ages, he might show the incomparable riches of his grace. (Ephesians 2:6)

Blessed are the pure in heart, for they shall see God. (Matthew 5:8)

Beloved, we are God's children now. What we do know is this: when he is revealed, we will be like him, for we will see Him as He is. (1 John 3:2)

 Notes for reflection

Can Animals Sin?

Can animals sin? "Yes," but "no." They can do sinful things like stealing and killing, but it doesn't seem to affect their future destiny. They are not made in "the image of God," and Christ did not die for their sin as He did for ours.

On the other hand, God created animals, and they are part of His beautiful creation. Will our pets and other animals be with us in heaven? Along with rivers, trees of life, and buildings, most scholars agree that animals will be present in heaven, glorifying God each in their respective way. Pray that your favorite dog or cat will be there, enjoying heaven along with you!

Isaiah shows this picture of heaven: "The wolf will dwell with the lamb, and the leopard will lie down with the young goat, and the calf and the lion and the yearling together; and a little child will lead them. The cow will feed with the bear, their young will lie down together, and the lion will eat straw like the ox. The infant will play near the cobra's den, and the young child will put his hand into the viper's nest. They will neither harm nor destroy on all my holy mountain, for the earth will be filled with the knowledge of the Lord as the waters cover the sea." (Isaiah 11:6-9)

No good thing will He withhold from those who walk uprightly. (Psalm 84:11)

Then I heard every creature in heaven and on earth and under the earth and on the sea, and all that is in them, saying: "To him who sits on the throne and to the Lamb be praise and honor and glory and power, forever and ever!" (Revelation 5:13)

For nothing will be impossible with God. (Luke 1:37)

Alzheimer's, Dementia, and Getting into Heaven

What happens to Christians who become demented? Half of the people over 85 experience confusion. Some become so confused that their personalities change, and they seem like a different person. They often stop praying. Do they still go to heaven?

God knows each person's heart at salvation. He seals our salvation with the filling of the Holy Spirit. The Bible assures us that the Holy Spirit is a deposit and a guarantee that every child of God will go to heaven at death. Confusion, dementia, and mental illness cannot negate or chase away the Holy Spirit guarantee. Demented folks are safely in heaven because of the Holy Spirit. Praise the Lord!

Therefore, if anyone is in Christ, the new creation has come. The old has gone; the new is here! (2 Corinthians 5:17)

When you believed, you were marked in him with a seal, the promised Holy Spirit, who is a deposit guaranteeing our inheritance until the redemption of those who are God's possession. (Ephesians 1:13,14)

For I am convinced that neither death nor life, neither angels nor demons, neither the present nor the future, nor any powers, neither height nor depth, nor anything else in all creation, will be able to separate us from the love of God that is in Christ Jesus our Lord. (Romans 8:38,39)

I am sure of this that he who began a good work in you will bring it to completion at the day of Jesus Christ. (Philippians 1:6)

Jesus Christ will sustain you to the end, guiltless in the day of our Lord Jesus Christ. God is faithful. (1 Corinthians 1:8,9)

Traveling is Exciting

Why do we all like to travel? Here is one reason: it's the closest we humans can get towards being omnipresent. God is "omnipresent"; that is, He is everywhere at all times. That, I think, would be fun and liberating. We could be at our favorite spot whenever we wanted. After that, we could zoom literally to another favorite location. We could experience wherever, whenever we wanted to. Just "beam up!"

God is everywhere at the same time. That concept is difficult for our finite minds to understand, but that's how God is; He's omnipresent. We, unfortunately, occupy only one place at a time. That's so restrictive, cumbersome, and boring at times. However, there is a "partial remedy" to our not being omnipresent. TRAVEL!

Go and experience another place; go anywhere you haven't been before. Visit a zoo, sit in the woods, or go for a walk. See the inside of someone else's house. Travel the world!

Want to be omnipresent? Remembering our travel is the closest we can get because we can only exist in one location at a time. However, you can also travel by your imagination while reading a book or go back in time by visiting a museum. That's about the best we can do.

Take heart, though; it will get much easier to travel once we get to heaven! After rising from the dead, Jesus could travel at will, appear, disappear, and go through walls. Yet He could eat and speak and be touched without pain or fatigue. We all look forward to our "spiritual bodies" after we die. That will be exciting!

For our citizenship is in heaven, where the Lord Jesus Christ will transform our lowly body to be like His glorious body. (Philippians 3:20,21)

We are children of God, and it has not yet been revealed what we shall be, but we know that when He is revealed, we shall be like Him, for we shall see Him as He is. (1 John 3:2)

So will it be with the resurrection of the dead. The body is raised imperishable; it is raised in glory and in power; it is raised a spiritual body. (1 Corinthians 15:42-44)

"Can a man hide himself in secret places so that I cannot see him? Do I not fill heaven and earth?" declares the Lord. (Jeremiah 23:24)

 Notes for reflection

The Swoosh

You should look forward to your "swoosh"! That is the moment of death when you swoosh into eternity. It is a beautiful doorway into the most exciting life that is beyond imagination. It will be a glorious reunion with the Lord and with our loved ones.

Many people are afraid of the swoosh and don't even wish to discuss it. Some think dying is painful, but that is not such a concern now with comfort care and excellent pain medicine. But the best news is that Jesus' death and resurrection guarantee that His children will rise from the dead just as He did. Jesus said He would prepare a place for us, and He will come again and take us to be with Him.

Three things seem to increase people's anticipation regarding the swoosh:

1. The deeper in love with the Lord we get.

2. The older we get.

3. The more pain we experience.

With great anticipation, you should look forward to your swoosh escorted by Jesus to the heavenly home built for you.

God so loved the world that He gave His only Son that whosoever believes in Him shall not perish but have everlasting life. (John 3:16)

Do not let your hearts be troubled. You believe in God, believe also in me. My Father's house has many rooms; I am going there to prepare a place for you. And if I go and prepare a place for you, I will come back and take you to be with me that you also may be where I am. (John 14:1-3)

Surely your goodness and love will follow me all the days of my life, and I will dwell in the house of the Lord forever. (Psalm 23:6)

"What no eye has seen, what no ear has heard, and what no human mind has conceived" —the things God has prepared for those who love him. (1 Corinthians 2:9)

You make known to me the path of life; you will fill me with joy in your presence, with eternal pleasures at your right hand. (Psalm 16:11)

 Notes for reflection

Is There a Second Chance?

Could there possibly be a second chance to become a Christian after death? Many people wish for another opportunity to make a choice. Unfortunately, the Bible doesn't present that as a possibility, so don't risk your eternity on it!

Here are some past scenarios regarding second chances. Adam and Eve were required to leave the garden after one tasty sin; no second chance. The Israelites received a second chance to enter the Promised Land 40 year later, but only after everybody in the first group died. Ananias and Sapphira fell dead after one misstatement.

It seems too risky to hope for a second chance to become a Christian after you die. Don't bet your life in eternity on that one. For heaven's sake, but more importantly, for your own sake, accept Jesus now. Here is how: #1. Ask Jesus for the forgiveness of your sins. #2. Ask Jesus to be Lord of your life. Now, without fear of hell, enjoy God's more abundant life that He has promised for you.

"Today is the day for Salvation," I tell you, now is the time of God's favor, now is the day of salvation. (2 Corinthians 6:2)

People are destined to die once, and after that, to face judgment. (Hebrews 9:27) Then they will go away to eternal punishment, but the righteous to eternal life. (Matthew 25:46)

If you declare with your mouth, "Jesus is Lord," and believe in your heart that God raised him from the dead, you will be saved. (Romans 10:9)

I have come that they may have life and have it to the full. (John 10:10b)

You make known to me the path of life; you will fill me with joy in your presence, with eternal pleasures at your right hand. (Psalm 16:11)

Famous Last Words

What are the last words you would like to say before you die? The very best four words are, "Jesus, I Love You." Can you imagine dying after you prayed those four words? That would look great on your resume!

Here are the final words of famous people:

Sir Winston Churchill (1874–1965) *I'm bored with it all.*

Diana, Princess of Wales (1961–1997) *My God. What's happened?*

John Lennon (1940–1980) *I'm shot.*

Sixty-three percent of all death row inmates have used "love" as the most common word in their last statements.

Practice praying "Jesus, I love you" often. This prayer and all prayers are stored in heaven for eternity. When you get there, you will find your prayers on the golden altar in front of God's throne. Your last four words will give off a sweet, pleasant odor recorded for eternity; they will never disappear. You will enjoy seeing and smelling their sweet aroma when you get there!

The elders were holding golden bowls full of incense, which are the prayers of God's people. Another angel was given the prayers of all God's people on the golden altar in front of the throne. The smoke of the incense, together with the prayers of God's people, went up before God from the angel's hand. (Revelation 5:8, 8:3,4)

After breakfast, Jesus asked Simon Peter, "Simon son of John, do you love me more than these?" (John 21:15)

You must love the Lord your God with all your heart, all your soul, and all your mind. (Deuteronomy 6:5, Matthew 22:37, Mark 12:30, Luke 10:27)

Can We Trust God's Word?

How can we know that we will come to life again and go to heaven after we die? If God could adequately reassure us, would it help? What reassurances would we need?

#1 It would help prove God's credibility if God would predict what He was going to do hundreds of years before He did something. Only God could do that. Accurate prophecies predicting anything impossible would be compelling, like a virgin birth or being born in a small insignificant town.

#2 If God would personally come to earth and perform impossible miracles repeatedly, that would help prove His credibility. Miracles should also be seen by close relatives, friends, and even those who hate him, so people aren't biased to lie about it.

#3 If God Himself would come to earth, die and remain dead for at least three days, and then come back to life, it would be convincing. After rising from the dead, He should stick around for at least five weeks to prove to everyone, including family members, close friends, and hundreds of people, that it was Him.

#4 Some other requirements for God to accomplish might also be helpful. God should promise that He will always love us and never change His mind about loving us. That would decrease a lot of anxiety; nobody wants a commitment that later is changed or broken.

#5 It would be safest for us to be near Him in heaven and not isolated at a distant place far away from this loving God.

#6 It would be a superb deal from this God if we could get into heaven by doing something simple. If entrance into heaven costs millions of dollars or doing something impossible, most of us wouldn't make it.

We have God's reassurances in His Word that we come to life again and go to heaven!

Scholars believe there are more than 300 prophecies about Jesus in the Old Testament. The possibility that anyone would satisfy just eight of the prophecies was 1 in 10^{17}. (Stoner, Peter. "Science Speaks," Jesus Film Project, January 14, 2018)

God gave his one and only Son, Jesus, so that everyone who believes in him will not perish but have eternal life. (John 3:16)

Fellow Israelites, listen to this: Jesus of Nazareth was a man accredited by God to you by miracles, wonders, and signs, which God did among you through him. (Acts 2:22)

Jesus said to her, "I am the resurrection and the life. The one who believes in me will live, even though they die." (John 11:25)

My Father's house has many rooms. I go to prepare a place for you. I will come back and take you to be with me that you also may be where I am. (John 14:2,3)

If you declare with your mouth, "Jesus is Lord," and believe in your heart that God raised him from the dead, you will be saved. (Romans 10:9, Acts 16:31)

 Notes for reflection

Intimacy with God

"Intimacy with God" is a frightening topic for many. It may seem scary to be too close to someone, especially if they invade our private space. It's even more upsetting if the person is extremely powerful. Do you prefer to keep a certain distance from the Lord? Is it possible to get too close?

We are all quite comfortable with God's "transcendence"; that is, God is in Heaven, and we worship Him way up there. On the other hand, the disciples walked intimately with Jesus. The more they realized He was God, the more exciting the closeness became. At the Last Supper, John even put his head on the chest of Jesus; that seems really personal. Would you feel comfortable putting your head on Jesus' chest?

I often wake up at night and can't get back to sleep. At times, but far too rarely, I invite Jesus to lie down beside me. He also is wide awake; we don't have to talk. Sometimes I thank Him for just being with me and for the life He has given me. Sometimes He talks to me!

If you can't sleep at night and feel brave, ask Jesus to lie down right beside you. Move over a bit and give Him some space. See what happens in perhaps what might be the most significant part of your entire day!

Come near to God, and he will come near to you. (James 4:8)

For me, it is good to be near God. (Psalm 73:28)

Come to me all you who are weary and heavy laden, and I will give you rest. (Matthew 11:28)

And he who loves me will be loved by my Father, and I will love him and manifest myself to him. (John 14:21)

Come with me by yourselves to a quiet place and get some rest.
(Mark 6:31)

Notes for reflection

His Holy Name

"I Am" is the most powerful name in all creation; it is the name of God! We will be filled with wonder and amazement throughout eternity, learning more about the great "I Am."

"I Am" is translated as "Yahweh," which historically has been too holy to pronounce. Therefore, "Yahweh" was abbreviated as "YHWH." Even YHWH was too sacred to say carelessly, so the Jewish people changed it to "Adonai," which means "My Lord." Our English Bible translates Adonai to "LORD." YHWH (I Am) occurs 6,828 times in the Old Testament, and it speaks of God's self-existence, self-sufficiency, and supreme sovereignty.

"I AM" is 'present tense' meaning that God is totally in the past and the future as though they are happening right now. It is not "I Was," now "I Am," and in the future, "I Will Be." God is present in the past, present, and future as though time doesn't exist. Think of God as living outside of time, yet He can see and enter into the past, present, and future as though it is right now.

That is a difficult concept since we humans are limited to our time dimension. We need spiritual insight to understand it. The Bible is clear that God exists in our future and even knows our future thoughts! God also knows the exact number of days we will live. He is the great, "I Am!"

A strong word of caution is in order: it is dangerous to be careless with God's name! The Bible warns us to honor His Holy Name. We can look forward to being thrilled in heaven as the Lord reveals more about what His Name means!

Oh Lord, our Lord, how majestic is your name in all the earth! (Psalm 8:1)

God said to Moses, "I am who I am." (Exodus 3:14)

No one is like you, Lord; you are great, and your name is mighty in power. (Jeremiah 10:6)

You shall not misuse the name of the Lord your God, for the Lord will not hold anyone guiltless who misuses his name. (Exodus 20:7)

But do not forget this one thing, dear friends: With the Lord, a day is like a thousand years, and a thousand years are like a day. (2 Peter 3:8)

"I am the Alpha and the Omega," says the Lord God, "who is, and who was, and who is to come, the Almighty." (Rev. 1:8)

Before a word is on my tongue, you, Lord, know it completely. Your eyes saw my unformed body; all the days ordained for me were written in your book before one of them came to be. (Psalm 139:4,16)

 **Notes for reflection**

Honor God's Name

God's name is powerful beyond words: I AM, Yahweh, YHWH, Adonai, LORD. We can't imagine the power in that Name! Number three of the Ten Commandments has this caution: "Do not take the name of the Lord in vain." In other words, do not use God's name as a swear word.

To dishonor God's name in any way is to offend Him. Do we not understand that He is Almighty God and worthy of our most profound praise and respect? The Bible says that we should "fear" God. The Jewish community put to death anyone who misused the Lord's name. Those who follow the Lord do not want to offend Him because we love Him.

If you hear someone use God's name as a swear word, silently save their life! Immediately pray to ask God's forgiveness for that person who disobeyed the Third Commandment. Pray for God's mercy, for they do not know what they are doing. Forgiveness is a beautiful thing, a gift from JHWH to keep us clean. The Holy Spirit can use your prayer for great good and prevent the person from falling into greater sin.

Now, what should we do with "gosh," "golly," "jeez," "jeepers"? Here is the Bible's answer: "Above all, my brothers and sisters, do not swear—not by heaven or by earth or by anything else. All you need to say is a simple "Yes" or "No." Otherwise, you will be condemned." (James 5:12)

Whoever blasphemes the name of the Lord shall surely be put to death. (Leviticus 24:13)

You shall not misuse the name of the Lord your God, for the Lord will not hold anyone guiltless who misuses his name. (Exodus 20:7)

If we confess our sins, he is faithful and just and will forgive us our sins and purify us from all unrighteousness. (1 John 1:9)

These are the ones I look on with favor: those who are humble and contrite in spirit and who tremble at my word. (Isaiah 66:2)

What is God Harvesting from You?

What does "harvest" mean in the Bible? Jesus told them, "The harvest is plentiful, but the workers are few. Ask the Lord of the harvest, therefore, to send out workers into his harvest field. Go!" (Luke 10:2,3, Matthew 9:37,38)

We immediately think that the harvest is sharing the Good News about Jesus Christ and encouraging people into the Kingdom of God; no one can argue with that. The Lord would like to bring in a large crop of new believers.

The "harvest crops," however, are much more than just conversions. A big crop that God harvests is your love; call them "love units" if you will. When you say, "I love you, Jesus," it becomes a harvest item that Jesus particularly likes. God also harvests each "thanks" that you send to Him. Another superb harvest crop is "praise."

Sometimes we have seasons of despair when we feel there is no hope, yet we trust God. God harvests that small amount of trust we muster in challenging times. How are you doing growing crops that Jesus wants to harvest?

Are there any other crops that come to mind? Pray about your crops and see if you can increase the yield this week! Here are some "crop" verses.

I tell you, open your eyes and look at the fields! They are ripe for harvest. Even now, the one who reaps draws a wage and harvests a crop for eternal life. (John 4:35,36)

Let us not become weary in doing good, for at the proper time, we will reap a harvest if we do not give up. (Galatians 6:9)

Peacemakers who sow in peace reap a harvest of righteousness. (James 3:18)

Now he who supplies seed to the sower will enlarge the harvest of your righteousness. (2 Corinthians 9:10)

To him, who sits on the throne and to the Lamb, be praise and honor and glory and power, forever and ever." (Revelation 5:13 - Add in wisdom, majesty, and wealth also.)

The fruit of the Spirit is love, joy, peace, patience, kindness, goodness, faithfulness, gentleness, and self-control. (Galatians 5:22 - The Fruit of the Spirit is a great harvest)

 Notes for reflection

Two Ways to Do Everything

There are two ways to do everything. One way is eternally significant and of great value; the other way is okay but goes "poof." Here is the trick to make the difference. Whether doing the dishes or changing a dirty diaper, whatever the task is, just ask Jesus to join you in the job. Doing tasks "with Jesus" makes all the difference.

We generally ask Jesus to be with us before major events like marriage or going into surgery. Ask Him to join you in your mundane activities also. Then they may become much more fun with Him near you. Don't complain too much, though, or He might show you the puncture wounds in His hands.

Jesus enjoys being with you so much; that's why activities done with Jesus become eternally significant. Invite Him alongside while you work; this "practicing the presence" is an excellent form of prayer. If you desire to "go higher," perform the task as if you are doing it for Jesus. Washing the dishes for Jesus turns a dull job into an incredible event! If Jesus is not involved in your routine task, it's a "poof" for eternal significance.

In summary, there are two ways to do everything. One way amounts to nothing, no matter how significant the task may be. The other way "with Jesus" gets recorded for eternity and becomes an activity of great value, no matter how small a chore. It is 'out of this world,' you might say.

Whatever you do, whether in word or deed, do it all in the name of the Lord Jesus, giving thanks to God the Father through him. (Colossians 3:17)

Whatever you do, work at it with all your heart, as working for the Lord, not for human masters. (Colossians 3:23)

So whether you eat or drink or whatever you do, do it all for the glory of God. (1 Corinthians 10:31)

Serve wholeheartedly, as if you were serving the Lord, not people, because you know that the Lord will reward each one for whatever good they do. (Ephesians 6:7,8)

Truly I tell you, whatever you did for one of the least of these brothers and sisters of mine, you did for me. (Matthew 25:40)

Therefore, I tell you, whatever you ask for in prayer, believe that you have received it, and it will be yours. (Mark 11:24)

 Notes for reflection

Why Did God Make Us?

Why did God make us? That's an easy question, and the correct answer is "for God's glory." However, many of us are confused about what being made "for His glory" means. To glorify God is to give Him what He wants, which provides Him with great pleasure. We can readily understand pleasure from these synonyms: joy, happiness, satisfaction, fun. He made us to "glorify Him" and give Him pleasure.

Since we are each made in God's image, our desires are very similar to God's desires. We make decisions in life that will give us the most pleasure and joy, even though it may take lots of work to get to that final payoff.

Your mom may have conceived you for her joy and happiness. Here are four different levels of pleasure you could give to her: how would you rank these "pleasureful actions?" Here is my ranking order:

1. Say to your mom, "I love you!" – That ranks the highest.
2. Praise and thank her. - Pretty high.
3. Spend time with her. - A little lower.
4. Help her do work. - Slightly lower.

We do best pleasing God - giving Him glory - when we love Him with our heart, soul, mind, and strength. God is love, and He likes it when we love Him back. He also loves it when we give His love to others.

Here is a bucket of pleasureful things to do: "praise, thanksgiving, prayer, read His Word, help your neighbor," and so much more. What works best for you to please God?

Unfortunately, we can disappoint the Lord by a big bucket of other things: "ignore God, take His name in vain" and do all the opposite stuff above. For heaven's sake and more importantly, for your own sake, DON'T GO THERE!

What is impressive is that the more we love God, the more God loves us back. That is the beautiful "win/win" benefit of pleasing God. The better we get at loving God, the more love we receive back from God. With great delight, find out what pleases the Lord!

Live as children of light and find out what pleases the Lord. (Ephesians 5:8,10)

Live peaceful and quiet lives in all godliness and holiness. This is good and pleases God our Savior. (1 Timothy 2:2,3)

Do what pleases him. And this is his command: to believe in his Son, Jesus Christ, and to love one another as he commanded us. (1John 3:22-23)

Delight yourself in the Lord, and He will give you the desires of your heart. (Psalm 37:4)

Love the Lord your God with all your heart and with all your soul and with all your strength and with all your mind; and, love your neighbor as yourself. (Luke 10:27)

 **Notes for reflection**

God is Light!

"God is light." What a remarkable statement! Light is miraculous and fascinating. Did you know that nothing travels faster than light (186,000 miles per second) – except for prayer? Light exists in streams of tiny energy packets called photons, which travel in varying wavelengths. Each wavelength produces a different color in this order: red, orange, yellow, green, blue, purple, and violet. Those seven colors make up rainbows that God miraculously makes each time sunshine hits raindrops!

Light is incredible. How do you explain that when God mixes all the colors together, the light becomes transparent and colorless? There is so much more to say about light. Start by studying Einstein's famous equation ($E = MC^2$): energy equals mass times the speed of light multiplied by the speed of light. The internet is an excellent place to start. The Bible is a superb place to end.

God made light with its miraculous properties to teach us about Himself. What do you think about these "light" verses?

God is light; in him, there is no darkness at all. (1 John 1:5)

The Lord is my light and my salvation–whom shall I fear? (Psalm 27:1)

Your word is a lamp for my feet, a light on my path. (Psalm 119:105)

God, the King of kings and Lord of lords, lives in unapproachable light, whom no one has seen or can see. (1 Timothy 6:15,16)

Do you like the book cover picture depicting God's light?

Jesus said, "I am the light of the world. Whoever follows me will never walk in darkness but will have the light of life." (John 8:12)

You are all children of the light and children of the day. We do not belong to the night or the darkness. (1 Thessalonians 5:5)

You are the light of the world. Let your light shine before others that they may see your good deeds and glorify your Father in heaven. (Matthew 5:14-16)

 Notes for reflection

Let's Pay the Lord Back!

We are enormously indebted to the Lord for the great things He has done for each one of us. So how much do we owe? It is time to pay God back; let's get the debt canceled! Here is a short and incomplete list of what we each probably need to pay back:

1. Our parents and the love they gave to us.

     $1 million

2. Our miraculous bodies: complex brain, heart, etc.

     $1 billion

3. The earth, sun, and stars in the galaxies.

     $1 billion

4. Christ dying to take away our sins - if we ask.

     $10 billion

5. The entrance fee to get into heaven.

     $1 billion

6. The daily rent fee to stay in the mansions in heaven.

     $1 million/day for eternity

7. Unseen costs that are clarified in the small print.

     $1 million/day for eternity

So there is just a rough list of the charges we each owe; billions of dollars to the Lord. What an impossible task to pay it back! What should we do? Here's a suggestion regarding how we should start.

Scream this prayer: "LORD, PLEASE HAVE MERCY! We will never be able to pay you back!" Then become "poor in spirit," realizing a severe dependency on God.

Blessed are the poor in spirit (that is unable to pay God back) for theirs is the kingdom of heaven. (Matthew 5:3)

The free gift of God is eternal life in Christ Jesus our Lord. (Romans 6:23)

And forgive us our debts, as we also have forgiven our debtors. (Matthew 6:12)

Praise be to the Lord, for he has heard my cry for mercy. (Psalm 28:6)

Praise God for His JUSTICE, MERCY, and GRACE

God's **Justice**: We get what we deserve!

God's **Mercy**: We don't get what we deserve!

God's **Grace**: We get what we don't deserve!

He saved us, not because of righteous things we had done, but because of his mercy. (Titus 3:5)

But because of his great love for us, God, who is rich in mercy, made us alive with Christ. (Ephesians 2:4,5)

 Notes for reflection

God's Reward System

God's reward system is one of the least talked about benefits of being a Christian. Does God use a reward system? Our concern is the motive; we desire to do "good works" because of our love for the Lord, not so that we can gain a reward.

I agree with that thinking; however, there is a balance to be made from Scripture. The reward system controls most aspects of our lives, from school to baseball to jobs. It's how managers and bosses get selected. It is why we work hard to earn the reward of becoming successful. A's are better than B's; the fastest track star receives the trophy.

We may find it hard to discuss God's reward system because of the concern for pride, greed, and one-upmanship. Again, we desire to obey the Lord because of our love for Him, not just to get a reward. How is your balance between doing "good works" because of your love of the Lord versus laying up treasure in heaven?

Let me present some encouragement from Scripture for the reward system, and then you may determine your own balance regarding storing up "reward" treasures in heaven.

But store up for yourselves treasures in heaven, where moths and vermin do not destroy, and where thieves do not break in and steal. (Matthew 6:20)

For the Son of Man is going to come, and then he will reward each person according to what they have done. (Matthew 16:27)

Do not let your left hand know what your right hand is doing so that your giving may be in secret. Then your Father, who sees what is done in secret, will reward you. (Matthew 6:3,4)

The one who plants and the one who waters have one purpose, and they will each be rewarded according to their own labor. (1 Corinthians 3:8)

Because you know that the Lord will reward each one for whatever good they do. (Ephesians 6:8)

But as for you, be strong and do not give up, for your work will be rewarded. (2 Chronicles 15:7)

Whoever is kind to the poor lends to the Lord, and he will reward them for what they have done. (Proverbs 19:17)

Look, I am coming soon! My reward is with me, and I will give to each person according to what they have done. (Revelation 22:12)

And if you give even a cup of cold water to one of the least of my followers, you will surely be rewarded. (Matthew 10:42 NLT)

Blessed are you when people insult you, persecute you and falsely say all kinds of evil against you because of me. Rejoice and be glad, because great is your reward in heaven. (Matthew 5:11,12)

 Notes for reflection

The Reward in Heaven is a Mystery

The reward in heaven is an absolute mystery! Isn't that amazing? The Bible tells us to lay up treasure in heaven, but what does that mean? Some think the prize will be "crowns" we will lay down before Jesus when we arrive in heaven. After that, the crowns are gone, and everyone is equal. That's okay.

It's similar to Jesus' parable where all the workers got the same wages no matter how long they worked. Just to be in heaven and experience the Lord would be more than enough; the treasure is getting into heaven!

On the other hand, could the treasure somehow be experiencing the Lord and His glory differently? It is easy to speculate varieties of rewards in earthly terms: Would you prefer to live on the top floor of the mansion in heaven or next to the cafeteria on the first floor? Would you want to be closer to the Lord or further away?

For now, it is a mystery what the possible rewards might be in heaven for giving a cup of cold water to someone or putting an extra dollar into the offering plate. Speculation gets us nowhere. Great rewards go to the martyrs of the faith, but what are the rewards? It is mysterious and beyond our imagination as to what the treasure is.

The heavenly rewards could be equalized, so all receive the same, or they might be enlarging beyond our imagination for eternity! Because it's a great mystery, we will have to wait to find out. The rewards that the Lord promises are, for now, a great supernatural mystery!

But store up for yourselves treasures in heaven, where moths and vermin do not destroy, and where thieves do not break in and steal. (Matthew 6:20)

Those who were hired last worked only one hour, and you have made them equal to us who have borne the burden of the work and the heat of the day. But he answered one of them, "I am not unfair to you, friend.

Didn't you agree to work for one denarius?" (Matthew 20:12,13)

The one who sows righteousness reaps a sure reward. Whoever is kind to the poor lends to the Lord, and he will reward them for what they have done. (Proverbs 11:18, Proverbs 19:17)

Look, I am coming soon! My reward is with me, and I will give to each person according to what they have done. (Revelation 22:12)

Command them to do good, be rich in good deeds, and be generous and willing to share. In this way, they will lay up treasure for themselves as a firm foundation for the coming age so that they may take hold of the life that is truly life. (1 Timothy 6:18,19)

And if anyone gives even a cup of cold water to one of these little ones who is my disciple, truly I tell you, that person will certainly not lose their reward. (Matthew 10:42)

But as for you, be strong and do not give up, for your work will be rewarded. (2 Chronicles 15:7)

 Notes for reflection

What is God's Appearance?

What is God's appearance? I know what you are going to say, but I'm going to try even so. As a child, many of us imagine God looks like a white-haired grandpa figure. Later, Christians envision a beautiful throne with bright light, power, thunder, and lightning.

All our conceptions fail us at this point, and we generally give up trying to visualize God. We switch to seeing Jesus Christ as the perfect representation of how we should imagine Him. Most Christians stop there, and rightly so. Prayerfully, let's try to go a step further.

Non-Christians sometimes view God as the sum total of all creation. This is called "Pantheism" and is not the correct visualization of God. Instead, imagine God easily holding all creation (two trillion expanding galaxies according to scientists) in His hand like He is holding a basketball.

Moses probably had the most intimate experience of being close to God. His first experience was hearing God from the burning bush. Later, when placed in the cleft of the rock, he witnessed God passing by. Another intimate experience was on Mount Sinai when the Lord gave him the Ten Commandments on two different occasions.

Also, Moses met with God in the Tent of Meeting regularly. What do you think he saw in the tent when he went inside? For just a moment, try to imagine going with Moses into that tent right now. You may sit down on one of the two chairs by the small table; just wait there a bit until God's presence enters. In moments, you will experience God right there with you! Your shoes are off; your eyes are probably closed. You are quiet; no talking at this point. You are totally expectant and on high alert listening. It's quiet and then…!

Well, that's probably a picture of your prayer time today with the Lord! Did He show up? What was He like, and what did He say?

God called to him from within the bush, "Moses! Moses!" And Moses said, "Here I am." "Do not come any closer. Take off your sandals, for the place where you are standing is holy ground." At this, Moses hid his face because he was afraid to look at God. (Exodus 3:4-6)

As Moses went into the tent, the pillar of cloud would come down and stay at the entrance while the Lord spoke with Moses. The Lord would speak to Moses face to face, as one speaks to a friend. (Exodus 33:9-11)

The Son is the radiance of God's glory and the exact representation of his being, sustaining all things by his powerful word. (Hebrews 1:3)

But when you pray, go into your room, close the door and pray to your Father, who is unseen. Then your Father, who sees what is done in secret, will reward you. (Matthew 6:6)

 Notes for reflection

Is There "Money" Under Your Mattress?

Do you have "spiritual riches" hiding right under your mattress? Many folks are trudging along in spiritual stagnation when they could easily unleash the Lord's blessings into their lives. It is almost like a poor person having a million dollars under his mattress but still living in poverty. Why live in spiritual poverty when you could be thrilled with a more abundant life?

Unfortunately, many Christians are guilty of living the "poverty life" spiritually. God's promises are readily available to each of us, but they need to be reached for and claimed. We must make an effort to seek the Lord and "grow in Christ." It is the ultimate adventure! Salvation and "riches in Christ" are right under your mattress. The Lord desires to bless you, not impoverish you. Wake up, lift your mattress by praying, reading the Bible, and going to church. Why remain a poor person spiritually when God wants you to have His "more abundant life?"

Wake up, lift your mattress, see the storehouse and then pray to receive all that the Lord has for you!

You don't receive because you don't ask. (James 4:2)

Ask, and it will be given to you; seek, and you will find; knock, and the door will be opened to you. For everyone who asks receives; the one who seeks finds; and to the one who knocks, the door will be opened. (Matthew 7:7,8)

Bring the whole tithe into the storehouse, that there may be food in my house. Test me in this, says the Lord Almighty, and see if I will not throw open the floodgates of heaven and pour out so much blessing that there will not be room enough to store it. (Malachi 3:10)

I pray that out of his glorious riches, he may strengthen you with power through his Spirit in your inner being so that Christ may dwell in your hearts through faith. Now to him who is able to do immeasurably more than all we ask or imagine, according to his power that is at work within us. (Ephesians 3:16-20)

I know your afflictions and your poverty—yet you are rich! (Revelation 2:9)

True godliness with contentment is great wealth. (1 Timothy 6:6)

I have come that you might have life, life more abundant. (John 10:10b)

 Notes for reflection

Becoming Rich, Powerful, and Famous

It seems as if there is a universal drive to become rich, powerful, and famous. Most people want more money so they can become happier. They think the more money you have, the happier you will be. After people become rich, they want more power, and after getting more power, they desire to become famous. How are you coming in your struggle to become rich, powerful, and famous?

Most folks work so hard their entire lives to acquire more and more. As followers of Jesus, we should strive to be different because we can find better contentment and power in the Christ-filled life. We are well-known to the Creator of the universe, and when we get to heaven, each of us will be rich, powerful, and famous! We will be wealthy: walking golden streets and wearing beautiful clothes of righteousness. We will have tremendous power to do whatever. Lastly, as God's children, we will be "well-known." If we have maximum riches, power, and fame in heaven, why struggle so hard to get them now? They will come soon enough.

Now is the time to focus on other "essentials." What then shall we do for a lifetime on earth? Consider these possibilities:

- Max out on love.
- Fill up on "fruit of the Spirit."
- Unleash the "incomparable power" of God.
- Harvest delicious fruit.

Love the Lord your God with all your heart and with all your soul and with all your strength and with all your mind; and, love your neighbor as yourself. (Luke 10:27)

The fruit of the Spirit is love, joy, peace, patience, kindness, goodness, faithfulness, gentleness, and self-control. (Galatians 5:22,23)

I pray that you may know his incomparably great power for us who believe. That power is the same as the mighty strength he exerted when he raised Christ from the dead and seated him at his right hand in the heavenly realms. (Ephesians 1:18-20)

I am the vine; you are the branches. If you remain in me and I in you, you will bear much fruit; apart from me, you can do nothing. (John 15:5)

 **Notes for reflection**

"None's" Need the Love of God

God Is Love! Fewer and fewer people believe it these days, it seems. The "None's" are the fastest-growing "religion" in the USA. These are people that check off "None" to denote their faith. The None's admit they have no religion or church affiliation; to them, God is small or nonexistent.

How can God show the None's that He loves them? Their eyes are blind, and their ears are deaf, their hearts are dead to God. What more can God possibly do to show these people that HE IS LOVE?

He has given each of the None's a body with life and a future with the freedom to choose to accept God's love.

It is incredible!

He has given None's Jesus, His Son, to die for each one at a great expense beyond our imagination.

It is incredible!

He has promised None's a more abundant life with supernatural help to live in inexpressible and glorious joy.

It is incredible!

He has placed eternity in everyone's heart, created heavens that day after day give forth speech, and has given His Word to tell all the None's about His love.

It is incredible!

He has promised None's eternity in the presence of God with pleasures forevermore.

It is incredible!

One thing remains: For God to show Himself face to face in all of His glory. At that moment, every knee will bow, and every tongue confess "Jesus Is Lord!" And at that moment, God's love and light and beauty and holiness and wisdom and power and majesty and wealth will be supernaturally incredible beyond imagination.

Many will stay close to God to experience His supernatural love for eternity. Others will not be allowed because of blindness, deafness, and hearts that were dead to God's incredible love poured out to them.

I, Jesus, have come that they may have life and have it more abundantly. (John 10:10b)

You love him, believe in him, and are filled with inexpressible and glorious joy, for you are receiving the end result of your faith, the salvation of your souls. (1 Peter 1:8,9)

You make known to me the path of life; you will fill me with joy in your presence, with eternal pleasures at your right hand. (Psalm 16:11)

And without faith, it is impossible to please God because anyone who comes to him must believe that he exists and that he rewards those who earnestly seek him. (Hebrews 11:6)

At the name of Jesus, every knee should bow, in heaven and on earth and under the earth and every tongue acknowledge that Jesus Christ is Lord. (Philippians 2:10,11)

Anyone whose name was not found written in the book of life was thrown into the lake of fire. (Revelation 20:15)

Notes for reflection

Oh, For Just a Little More!

Oh, for just a little more! Wouldn't you like a little more? But more of what? Most of us are stuck trying to get a bit more money to achieve happiness.

Instead of pursuing a little more money, however, switch to seeking God and doing His will during these short years on planet earth. Then you most likely will find true happiness, and God will supply everything that you seriously need. Here are some promises from God explaining His goals for your true happiness.

Seek first the Kingdom of God and be right with Him, and all these things will be added. (Matthew 6:33)

The Lord is my shepherd; I shall lack nothing. (Psalm 23:1)

My God will meet all your needs according to the riches of his glory in Christ Jesus. (Philippians 4:19)

What good will it be for someone to gain the whole world yet forfeit their soul? (Matthew 16:26)

No one can serve two masters; for either he will hate the one and love the other, or else he will be loyal to the one and despise the other. You cannot serve God and mammon. (Matthew 6:24)

Praise be to the God and Father of our Lord Jesus Christ! In his great mercy, he has given us an inheritance that can never perish, spoil, or fade. This inheritance is kept in heaven for you. (1 Peter 1:3,4)

This is what the Lord says: "Let not the wise boast of their wisdom or the strong boast of their strength or the rich boast of their riches, but let the one who boasts boast about this: that I am the Lord, who exercises kindness, justice, and righteousness on earth, for in these I delight," declares the Lord. (Jeremiah 9:23,24)

You believe in Jesus and are filled with an inexpressible and glorious joy, for you are receiving the end result of your faith, the salvation of your souls. (1 Peter 1:8,9)

 Notes for reflection

Turn Hay into Gold

The Bible talks about "hay, wood and stubble" and "silver and gold" activities. Hay, wood, and stubble activities get burned up and amount to nothing. When tested in the fire, silver and gold activities get purer and are of great value.

I have many hay, wood, and stubble activities but would like to do better. How can you and I change the "hay stuff" into silver and gold? Here is how we can improve without changing too much!

If we invite Jesus during our hay, wood, and stubble activities, He will be enjoying them with us. Invite Jesus to enjoy your ice cream cone or your walk. That will please the Lord and will turn eating an ice cream cone or a walk into gold. If you are watching TV, just invite the Lord to be with you. If you decide to do nothing, ask Jesus to do nothing with you. There is more gold. Be a billionaire in Heaven!

For really high yield gold mining, love God with all your heart, soul, mind, and strength. Loving your neighbor now and then works well also. Specialize in turning hay, wood, and stubble activities into silver, gold, and fantastic treasure!

For no one can lay any foundation other than the one already laid, which is Jesus Christ. If anyone builds on this foundation using gold, silver, costly stones, wood, hay, or straw, their work will be shown for what it is. It will be revealed with fire, and the fire will test the quality of each person's work. If what has been built survives, the builder will receive a reward. If it is burned up, the builder will suffer loss but yet will be saved—even though only as one escaping through the flames. (1 Corinthians 3:11-15)

If you do not remain in me, you are like a branch that is thrown away and withers; such branches are picked up, thrown into the fire, and burned. (John 15:6)

Jesus replied: "Love the Lord your God with all your heart and with all your soul and with all your mind. This is the first and greatest commandment. And the second is like it: Love your neighbor as yourself. (Matthew 22:37-39)

 Notes for reflection

Choose to Become a Spiritual Eye Doctor

Choose to become a spiritual eye doctor. Eye doctors (ophthalmologists) help people to see clearly with excellent vision. They do vision checks, fit people with glasses, perform cataract surgery, and much more.

Many people these days have a severe "spiritual vision" problem. Those who are spiritually nearsighted can't see heaven. Those with farsighted spiritual vision can't focus on what the Lord is doing right in front of them. With spiritual cataracts, most can't read the Bible. With "floaters," they drift in and out of the church, but everything is a bit fuzzy. With poor night vision, people get into big trouble after midnight.

To become a good spiritual eye doctor, all you have to do is help the people around you to see better. Here's your initial job description; help people to make a choice:

1. Choose heaven with inexpressible joy, thrill, and adventure forever.

OR

2. Choose hell with total darkness and pain for eternity.

Many people choose the second one because of vision problems. You can help the people where you live or become a missionary traveling overseas to remove people's blindness. Are there people with severe vision problems near to you? It's exciting and rewarding to be a spiritual eye doctor. You can do it!

Satan, who is the god of this world, has blinded the minds of those who don't believe. They are unable to see the glorious light of the Good News. They don't understand this message about the glory of Christ. (2 Corinthians 4:4)

See, darkness covers the earth, and thick darkness is over the peoples. (Isaiah 60:2)

You can enter God's Kingdom only through the narrow gate. The highway to hell is broad, and its gate is wide for the many who choose that way. (Matthew 7:13)

Indeed the "right time" is now. Today is the day of salvation. (2 Corinthians 6:2)

Choose for yourselves this day whom you will serve, but as for me and my household, we will serve the Lord. (Joshua 24:15)

If you declare with your mouth, "Jesus is Lord," and believe in your heart that God raised him from the dead, you will be saved. (Romans 10:9)

Here I am! I stand at the door and knock. If anyone hears my voice and opens the door, I will come in and eat with that person, and they with me. (Revelation 3:20)

 Notes for reflection

Are You Afraid to Become a Follower of Jesus?

To become a Christian may seem scary to some folks. Asking Jesus to be "Lord of your life" sounds intimidating because there is a fear of losing control. That may be why many lack courage and are afraid to become a follower of Jesus. Others think life would be boring and not much fun. Satan has blinded many people's eyes to make things seem worse, so they can't see well enough to make the big decision.

As for me, I would be more afraid of not being a follower of Jesus. Once you become a Christian, you see things differently. Here are four benefits from the Bible to take away fear:

1. Inexpressible and glorious joy to the max.
2. Love, joy, and peace beyond what you can muster on your own.
3. You will be on the winning side.
4. Serious pleasures forever and ever throughout eternity.

I, Jesus, have come that they may have life and have it to the full. (John 10:10b)

The fruit of the Spirit is love, joy, peace, patience, kindness, goodness, faithfulness, gentleness, and self-control. (Galatians 5:22,23)

You believe in Jesus and are filled with inexpressible and glorious joy, for you are receiving the end result of your faith, the salvation of your souls. (1 Peter 1:8,9)

You, God, will fill me with joy in your presence, with eternal pleasures at your right hand. (Psalm 16:11)

"Lord Almighty" - 125 times in the Bible - GOD WINS!

No eye has seen, no ear has heard, no human mind has conceived—
the things God has prepared for those who love him. (1 Corinthians 2:9)

The Lord will guide you always. (Isaiah 58:11)

 Notes for reflection

Brave or Foolhardy?

David's story against Goliath or Moses' against Pharaoh would rank very high in a test for bravery. I am not very brave. I learned very early that running away was better than fighting someone big. It is crucially important to assess the strength of an opponent before making a challenge.

Although they may not realize it, some people are very foolish to "take on God." God is so big, so wise, so powerful. Yet, people want to fight God. They want to change Him into what they want their personal god to be! But, God is not weak, tired, or whimsical.

Nowadays, many people are creating their own "god." It is as though there is a "god buffet" out there where people can choose what god qualities would best fit their tastes. Many would like to improve on the God of the Bible by selecting an "always loving, never judgmental" god. Then they would get rid of hell and allow everyone to go to heaven or at the very least be annihilated after death.

God is almighty and all-powerful. We cannot change Him according to our whims and desires. Many people are very brave, or are they foolhardy? You cannot squeeze God into a small god who suits your fancy.

The ultimate adventure for each of us will be to grow "Closer to God" and get to know Him personally. The more we find out about God, the more amazed we will become with His awesomeness. An eternity of amazement awaits us!

The fool says in his heart, "There is no God." They are corrupt. (Psalm 14:1, 53:1)

For although they knew God, they neither glorified him as God nor gave thanks to him, but their thinking became futile, and their foolish hearts were darkened. (Romans 1:21)

See, darkness covers the earth, and thick darkness is over the peoples. (Isaiah 60:2)

I keep asking that God may give you the Spirit of wisdom and revelation so that you may know him better. (Ephesians 1:17)

Great is the Lord, and greatly to be praised, and his greatness is unsearchable. (Ps 145:3)

Jesus Christ is the same yesterday and today and forever. (Hebrews 13:8)

Come and see what God has done: he is awesome in his deeds toward the children of men. (Psalm 66:5)

 Notes for reflection

The Stakes are Huge!

The stakes of life are high, but it is easy to win! One easy choice is all it takes. We each start with one life, and everyone makes the "big choice."

Let me explain. If a millionaire gambles $100, it doesn't matter much if he loses it. On the other hand, if he gambles half of his total wealth, he is taking a significant risk for his future. If he gambles "all or nothing," he is taking an even greater risk.

Most gamblers would prefer to risk only a little at a time. In Christianity, it is "all or nothing." We might wish the stakes of life wouldn't be so high. We love the halfway spot with compromise and second chances forever. Unfortunately, that's not the way it is. We decide to be a Christian or not be a Christian; it's impossible to be partial Christian and partial non-Christian. While it is sometimes tricky for persons to know, God knows who has turned to Him and has become a follower of Jesus.

We may wish the stakes in this life wouldn't be so "all or none." Those stakes are enormous for each one of us! Many people are gambling their lives away for the god of money, fame, or other life distractions. We each get one life in which to follow Jesus.

It is an easy decision or a "no brainer" if one understands the incredible benefits of asking Jesus to be Lord of your life. It is not a risky, dangerous decision; it is a sure thing to win!

If you declare with your mouth, "Jesus is Lord" and believe in your heart that God raised him from the dead, you will be saved. (Romans 10:9)

What good will it be for someone to gain the whole world yet forfeit their soul? Or what can anyone give in exchange for their soul? (Matthew 16:26)

Though you have not seen him, you love him; and even though you do not see him now, you believe in him and are filled with an inexpressible and glorious joy. (1 Peter 1:8)

Command those who are rich in this present world not to be arrogant nor to put their hope in wealth, which is so uncertain, but to put their hope in God, who richly provides us with everything for our enjoyment. (1 Timothy 6:17)

 Notes for reflection

Which Religion Should I Choose?

There are so many religions from which to choose. Each religion claims that they are right and that the others are false. It is impossible to be a faithful follower with all of them since most are exclusive of the others. We could spend a lifetime studying and comparing religions. Here is my very shortened course regarding which of all the religions is the one to follow.

If you made your decision on which religions most people have chosen, you would look at world statistics for major religious groups:

- Christianity (31.2%)
- Islam (24.1%)
- Hinduism (15.1%)
- Buddhism (6.9%)
- Atheists, Agnostics (7%)

By 2050, It is predicted that Christianity will continue as the largest group with three billion followers, but Islam is increasing in number and will be a close second. The United States has the largest Christian population globally, followed by Brazil, Mexico, and Russia. China has the most atheists in the world.

Here are some of the objective factors to help you conclude that Christianity is the true faith:

- The fulfillment of Bible prophecy
- The scientific accuracy of the Bible
- The historical evidence for the Bible
- The miraculous interventions by God
- The confirmation of biblical narratives by archaeology
- The deaths of Jesus' disciples
- Your own relationship with God as He proves Himself to you while you seek Him

No other religious book comes even close to the Bible regarding its scientific and historical accuracy and the immense number of fulfilled prophecies. Biblical prophecy is particularly compelling; God predicts important future events before they occur. Christ's birth and death were prophesied 300 years before they happened. The Dead Sea Scrolls found 125 years after they were written around year 5 AD prove their validity.

The death and resurrection evidence of Jesus with biblical and non-biblical historians is confirmed. The forty days post-resurrection accounts by Jesus' close friends, mother, and brothers are robust evidence. All deaths of the disciples strongly verify their belief that Jesus was and is God.

We each need to make our own decision about this important question during our lifetime. The decision has crucial consequences not only during our earthly life but also for eternity "which is very, very long especially toward the end!" (Woody Allen)

For no prophecy was ever produced by the will of man, but men spoke from God as they were carried along by the Holy Spirit. (2 Peter 1:21)

All Scripture is breathed out by God and profitable for teaching, for reproof, for correction, and for training in righteousness. (2 Timothy 3:16)

Do your best to present yourself to God as one approved, a worker who has no need to be ashamed, rightly handling the word of truth. (2 Timothy 2:15)

 Notes for reflection

Is There a Way to Get Rid of Hell?

There must be a way to get rid of hell. If we could eliminate that threat, it might decrease some anxiety on earth. Many people fear death because they are concerned about what comes next.

Belief in an "afterlife" is nearly universal. Almost all religions, including Christianity, Hinduism, Islam, Buddhism, and ancestor worship, teach there will be an "afterlife" with a good or bad place to be sent after a judgment.

People in Western cultures have tried to get rid of hell. The most common strategy is to get rid of belief in a god; if there is no god, there cannot be a heaven or hell. Atheistic groups are increasing, it seems, and getting rid of hell is a large factor in their appeal.

God's plans are firm. It doesn't much matter what we think; heaven and hell still exist whether people believe it or don't believe it.

There is a simple solution to remove anxiety about hell; Jesus solved the problem. He loves us so much that He died on the cross and took our sins away. When Jesus rose from the grave, He went to heaven to prepare a place for His followers. When we die, we will also rise to be with Him in heaven forever. Don't be concerned; the Holy Spirit guarantees that a believer will not go to hell.

For God so loved the world that he gave his one and only Son, that whoever believes in him shall not perish but have eternal life. (John 3:16)

If you declare with your mouth, "Jesus is Lord," and believe in your heart that God raised him from the dead, you will be saved. (Romans 10:9)

Believe in the Lord Jesus, and you will be saved—you and your household. (Acts 16:31)

My Father's house has many rooms; I am going there to prepare a place for you. I will come back and take you to be with me so that you may be where I am. (John 14:2,3)

The Big Four!

The four most significant reasons people don't become Christians are:

#1 They think evolution and science disprove Genesis and the Bible.

#2 Bad things happen to good people, and the all-powerful God didn't prevent them; therefore, the loving God must not exist.

#3 Christian hypocrites prove that Christianity is bogus.

#4 People prefer for there not to be a God.

Here is my shortened take on the Big Four:

#1 Contemporary evolutionary theory agrees quite closely with Genesis if a "day" can be "ages." The point of disagreement is whether God created it or whether creation happened on its own without God.

#2 The Bible declares that God uses suffering for great good in our lives. Christ's death on the Cross for our benefit is the best example to consider in our suffering. Are difficulties a part of God's loving plan, although the reason for them may be unknown to us? Consider these two verses:

All things work together for good to those who love the Lord and are called according to His purpose. (Romans 8:28)

For our light and momentary troubles are achieving for us an eternal good which far outweighs them all. (2 Corinthians 4:17)

#3 Oops, please forgive us, Lord!

#4 This is a huge reason! Many people simply prefer God not to exist; then heaven and hell don't exist either. Many intellectuals work hard to prove their "theology." They like to run their own lives, and they don't want anyone—especially God—to interfere with the way they're living. In essence, they would prefer for themselves to be god instead of letting God be God.

The fool says in his heart; There is no God. (Psalm 14:1)

Take life easy; eat, drink, and be merry. But God said to him, "You fool! This very night, your life will be demanded from you". (Luke 12:19,20)

Be entirely trustworthy and good. Then they will make the teaching about God our Savior attractive in every way. (Titus 2:10)

You must worship Christ as Lord of your life. And if someone asks about your hope as a believer, always be ready to explain it. But do this in a gentle and respectful way. (1 Peter 3:15,16)

Let your conversation be always full of grace, seasoned with salt, so that you may know how to answer everyone. (Colossians 4:6)

 **Notes for reflection**

Good Deed Erasers - Do they Work?

Many people believe that "good deeds" will erase or balance out bad ones. For example, if you do something really bad, you can erase the consequences by doing something really good. Their theology is that doing good erases or cancels out bad.

What do you think about this? If you sin, put money into the offering plate, and then God will erase the sin. Or you could feed starving children or help an older adult cross the street. Some think that if you perform enough of these good deeds, they will balance out the bad as if on a weighing scale! If the scale shows more "good" than "bad" at the end of life, the person is okay. Are you convinced that good deeds erase the consequences of evil deeds?

Good deeds are splendid, but they are terrible "sin erasers." Doing good works" is excellent; however, they won't eliminate even a small sin.

Everyone sins; in fact, we are even born with sin. The amount doesn't matter so much. If we sin at all, we are in trouble with a holy God.

There is excellent news, though. There is an easy, inexpensive, fast solution to get rid of "sin tonnage!" Just confess your sins and say you are sorry. Do it now and get rid of all your sins!

If we confess our sins, he is faithful and just and will forgive us our sins and purify us from all unrighteousness. (1 John 1:9)

God's Fairness or God's Forgiveness?

Which do you prefer: God's "fairness" or God's "forgiveness"? "Fairness" sounds like a good idea until you realize you are a sinner. If you choose God's "fairness," you will be judged by His high standard. You might not like to see yourself in God's eyes; you will get what you deserve! If you have ever messed up, that could be a problem because God is very fair and just.

The choice between God's forgiveness and God's fairness isn't tough. Fall on your knees and beg God for His mercy and forgiveness. If God is fair, we won't be doing very well because we must be sinless. For Heaven's sake, but more importantly, for your own sake, immediately choose GOD'S FORGIVENESS!

Even though it is relatively easy for us to get rid of our sins, Jesus suffered greatly to make that possible. Take the only way to get rid of sin; ask Jesus to forgive it all now. Whew! That was easy!

If we claim we have no sin, we are only fooling ourselves and not living in the truth. But if we confess our sins to him, he is faithful and just to forgive us our sins and to cleanse us from all wickedness. (1 John 1:8,9)

For all have sinned and fall short of the glory of God. For the wages of sin is death, but the gift of God is eternal life in Christ Jesus, our Lord. (Romans 3:23, Romans 6:23)

The heart is deceitful above all things and beyond cure. Who can understand it? (Jeremiah 17:9)

God's **fairness** is getting what you deserve
God's **mercy** is not getting what you deserve
God's **Grace** is getting what you don't deserve

Which is Easier? Faith or No Faith?

Which is easier? To have faith that God exists or to have faith that God doesn't exist? I believe, without question, that it takes much more faith to believe there is no God. Here are some reasons:

God created science. Science proves God's existence and agrees with the Bible. Scientists often try to exclude God from being the cause of creation and scientific laws. Most scientists agree that the entire universe began with a big bang explosion from something the size of a hydrogen atom or even possibly out of nothing! Some modern-day scientists have difficulty giving God credit for creating what science has discovered.

The first two scientific examples below are from the human body and are so incredible that they prove God exists! The following five examples show that faith in God is more straightforward than believing that God doesn't exist.

#1 DNA is the intricate genetic material that gives each human body all the instructions needed for each individual. You received six feet of DNA from your father and six feet from your mother at your conception. If placed end to end, the DNA in your body would reach to the sun, 93 million miles, and back again for 186 million miles total. Only God can do that!

#2 The red blood cells in one human body would reach around the world two and one-half times at the equator, over 62,000 miles if placed side by side. Only God can make each body so miraculously complicated to create DNA and red blood cells this perfectly. It's not possible with evolutionary theory. These are two examples out of countless others where science proves that only God could do that!

#3 God is love. Morality requires God, whether you're religious or not. Evolution has no answer for our high level of human character. A devotion to help or even die for others, including enemies, is a Biblical morality not possible by evolution.

#4 God is light. Light is miraculous to be transparent but made up of multiple colors (red, orange, yellow, green, blue, violet) when focussed through a prism. There are so many other miraculous pieces of evidence everywhere in creation with rainbows, sunsets, clouds, etc.

#5 There is a sense of "eternity in the hearts" of humans. Almost all people throughout the history of humanity have an inner knowledge that a god or gods exist. Generally, all religions believe that there is life after death.

#6 Christian funeral services are different from non-Christian funerals. Christian funerals often are "celebrations" because the deceased has gone to be with the Lord in heaven. Although grieving the loved one's loss, followers of Jesus have a sense of peace, knowing the family will be united together again in heaven.

#7 Sometimes, society inadvertently promotes the validity of Christianity. Many people swear using God's name or Jesus Christ's name in vain. Tragically, we hear cursing more and more in public these days. One never hears swearing-in Buddha's name, Ganesh's name (Hindu), or Allah's name.

God does not force belief in himself, although He could. Instead, he has provided sufficient proof of His existence to respond to him. Faith in God is compelling from the "miraculous" to the "common sense" to the "inner knowing." Our faith in God will increase as we see and understand more of what God has created!

Now, are you aware of any good evidence that God does not exist?

What may be known about God is plain because God has made it plain to them. For since the creation of the world, God's invisible qualities—his eternal power and divine nature—have been clearly seen, being understood from what has been made, so that people are without excuse. For although they knew God, they neither glorified him as God nor gave thanks to him, but their thinking became futile, and their foolish hearts were darkened. (Romans 1:19-21)

And without faith, it is impossible to please God because anyone who comes to him must believe that he exists and that he rewards those who earnestly seek him. (Hebrews 11:6)

In the beginning, God created the heavens and the earth. (Genesis 1:1)

God is love. Whoever lives in love lives in God, and God in them. (1 John 4:8,16)

He has made everything beautiful in its time. He has also set eternity in the human heart. (Ecclesiastes 3:11)

Do not let your hearts be troubled. You believe in God; believe also in me. My Father's house has many rooms; I am going there to prepare a place for you. I will come back and take you to be with me that you also may be where I am. (John 14:1-3)

 Notes for reflection

Our Sun Blows Up in Five Billion Years!

Scientists have calculated that the universe as we know it today, is expanding. If they estimate the expansion speed and play it backward, they estimate that the entire universe started 13.8 billion years ago with a big bang out of a hydrogen atom or even out of nothing! That fits perfectly with Genesis if each day can be "eons" of time. Otherwise, seven "days" still works, putting creation around 8000 years ago.

Scientists estimate our sun will implode about 5 billion years from now. That means that it will cool down, shrink into itself, and when it gets small enough, it will explode. Earth obviously will be gone as we know it.

Let's just go with God and be His church, the Bride of Christ, so that where He goes, we go also. God has prepared an eternal, wonderfully safe place for us. God wins in the beginning, middle, and end, so we'll be on the winning side throughout eternity. There is just so little to worry about when you are a follower of Jesus!

In the beginning, God created the heavens and the earth. (Genesis 1:1)

"I am the Alpha, and the Omega" says the Lord God, "who is, and who was, and who is to come, the Almighty." (Revelation 1:8)

For in him, all things were created: things in heaven and on earth, visible and invisible, whether thrones or powers or rulers or authorities; all things have been created through him and for him. (Colossians 1:16)

I form the light and create darkness, I bring prosperity and create disaster; I, the Lord, do all these things. (Isaiah 45:7)

I make known the end from the beginning, from ancient times, what is still to come. I say, "My purpose will stand, and I will do all that I please." (Isaiah 46:10)

How much Power does God have?

How much power does God have? Let's start with the Big Bang and all of creation, which is expanding and getting bigger and bigger by His power. That includes trillions of galaxies with black holes and explosions, etc. It's all created with His power.

The sun radiates 330 trillion horsepower of energy to the earth's surface daily. The total energy the sun emits in a single second is greater than the amount of energy the human race has consumed throughout its entire history. The earth intercepts about two billionths of the energy being generated by the sun at any given time. That is nothing compared to God's power!

God has infinite power! That is, there is no limit to the power available for Him to use. When we are in heaven, we will be worshipping God "Almighty." "Almighty" means that all authority is His, and there is no limit to His power. Throughout eternity we will be amazed at the display of God's incredible power.

Some of God's incredible power is available to you! Have you figured out how to unleash it?

Be strong in the Lord and in his mighty power. (Ephesians 6:10)

I pray that the eyes of your heart may be enlightened in order that you may know his incomparably great power for us who believe. That power is the same as the mighty strength he exerted when he raised Christ from the dead. (Ephesians 1:18-20)

With Christ, you were raised to new life because you trusted the mighty power of God, who raised Christ from the dead. (Colossians 2:12)

Holy, Holy, Holy is the Lord God, the Almighty. (Revelation 4:8)

Forever since the world was created, people have seen the earth and sky. Through everything God made, they can clearly see his invisible qualities, his eternal power, and divine nature. So, they have no excuse for not knowing God. (Romans 1:20)

Lord God! It is you who have made the heavens and the earth by your great power and by your outstretched arm! Nothing is too hard for you. (Jeremiah 32:17)

How great is our Lord! His power is absolute! (Psalm 147:5)

We can't imagine the greatness of his power. (Job 37:5)

 Notes for reflection

Pray for the Impossible!

As you "magnify" the Lord and He becomes more significant and more powerful in your life, try praying for the impossible! Don't limit God with only small prayer requests; He may desire for you to pray for a miracle that will bring Him great glory. Start by praying for God's guidance about what to pray, then keep your spiritual eyes open for divine appointments from Him and tremendous answers to your prayers.

Is it scriptural to pray for the impossible? The Word of God encourages us to think and pray big, then watch and see what He will do. Pray with these verses as you pray for the impossible!

Ask, and it will be given to you; seek, and you will find; knock, and the door will be opened to you. For everyone who asks receives; the one who seeks finds; and to the one who knocks, the door will be opened. (Matthew 7:7,8)

Now to Him who is able to do immeasurably beyond what we think or imagine according to His power that works in us. (Ephesians 3:20)

Very truly I tell you, whoever believes in me will do the works I have been doing, and they will do even greater things than these. And I will do whatever you ask in my name, so that the Father may be glorified in the Son. You may ask me for anything in my name, and I will do it. (John 14:11-14)

You do not have because you do not ask God. (James 4:2)

Truly I tell you, if you have faith as small as a mustard seed, you can say to this mountain, "Move from here to there," and it will move. Nothing will be impossible for you. (Matthew 17:20)

Jesus looked at them and said, "With man, this is impossible, but with God all things are possible." (Matthew 19:26)

Take delight in the Lord, and he will give you the desires of your heart. (Psalm 37:4)

 **Notes for reflection**

The Big "Why"?

There are two questions, "how" and "why." What is the big deal about the "why" question?

The big deal is that science is unable to answer the "why" question. Science does try to answer the "how" question. Two favorite "how" questions scientists love to answer are:

1. How did God create the universe?
2. How did God create humans?

But science is unable to answer the two far bigger questions;

1. Why did God create the universe?
2. Why did God create humans?

One concern is that when scientists figure out how God created something, they may erroneously conclude that God didn't create it. They often remark that it occurred "naturally according to evolutionary principles" instead of God causing the process according to His laws. Always remember that God made science, and science supports God.

God has the answer to the big "why" question in life!

Worthy are you, our Lord and God, to receive glory and honor and power, for you created all things, and by your will, they existed and were created. (Revelation 4:11)

For by him all things were created: things in heaven and on earth, visible and invisible, whether thrones or powers or rulers or authorities; all things were created by him and for him. (Colossians 1:16)

The heavens declare the glory of God; the skies proclaim the work of his hands. Day after day, they pour forth speech; night after night, they reveal knowledge. (Psalm 19:1,2)

The Lord, your God, is with you, he is mighty to save. He will take great delight in you, he will quiet you with his love, he will rejoice over you with singing. (Zephaniah 3:17)

I have made them for my glory. It was I who created them. (Isaiah 43:7)

 Notes for reflection

Pascal's Philosophical "Choice"

Blaise Pascal (1623-1662) offered a common-sense reason for believing in God. He argued that the potential benefits of believing in God are vast; on the other hand, not believing is risky and dangerous.

Pascal postulates that each human bets with their life regarding whether God exists or does not exist. He argues that a rational person should live as though God exists and seek to believe in God. Here is his logical reasoning:

If you bet your life that God exists and believe in Him, you gain heaven. You win!

If you bet your life that God doesn't exist, and He does exist, you gain hell. You lose big time!

If you bet your life that God doesn't exist, and He doesn't exist, it doesn't matter what you believe if there is no God.

Pascal says we each make this decision about whether or not God exists during our lifetime. He argues that it is much safer to believe in God, resulting in infinite gains in heaven. He says it is very dangerous not to believe in God. Belief in God gains everything and prevents losing everything.

Becoming a follower of Jesus is so much more than Pascal's simple logical argument, but his view is a beginning place for some.

The fool says in his heart, "There is no God." (Psalm 14:1, Psalm 53:1)

You make known to me the path of life; you will fill me with joy in your presence, with eternal pleasures at your right hand. (Psalm 16:11)

And I saw the dead, great and small, standing before the throne, and books were opened. Another book was opened, which is the book of life. The dead were judged according to what they had done as recorded in the books. Anyone whose name was not found written in the book of life was thrown into the lake of fire. (Revelation 20:12,15)

Existentialism Exposed

What all Existentialists have in common, according to Sartre, is the view that God does not exist, and so everything is permitted. Soren Kierkegaard (1813-1855), the father of Existentialism, stressed that each of us is alive, and we have the freedom to make choices. These choices may give us personal meaning in our lives despite living in an irrational universe with suffering and death.

Existentialism is about you being your own hero; you are your personal god. Anybody can do whatever they want to do, and there are no rules. Without God, lives have no inherent meaning or purpose. Therefore, the only way to counter this nothingness is to embrace your own existence and choices.

In summary, Existentialists believe that we are born without purpose into a world that makes no sense. However, each person has the freedom to create his or her personal sense of meaning in this irrational universe with ultimate death.

The fool says in his heart, "There is no God." (Psalm 14:1) Here is a Ruppian translation of Psalm 14:1: A foolish philosophy says out loud, "There is no God."

See to it that no one takes you captive through hollow and deceptive philosophy, which depends on human tradition and the elemental spiritual forces of this world rather than on Christ. (Colossians 2:8)

For we are God's handiwork, created in Christ Jesus to do good works, which God prepared in advance for us to do. (Ephesians 2:10)

See what great love the Father has lavished on us, that we should be called children of God! (1 John 3:1)

And so we know and rely on the love God has for us. God is love. Whoever lives in love lives in God, and God in them. (1 John 4:16)

"For I know the plans I have for you," declares the Lord, "plans to prosper you and not to harm you, plans to give you hope and a future." (Jeremiah 29:11)

For God so loved the world that he gave his one and only Son, that whoever believes in him shall not perish but have eternal life. (John 3:16)

For I am convinced that neither death nor life nor anything else in all creation will be able to separate us from the love of God that is in Christ Jesus our Lord. (Romans 8:37-39)

 Notes for reflection

Postmodernism Explained

Postmodernism is an ideology that is prominent in our society today. It is characterized by relativism and skepticism, a general suspicion of reason. In postmodernism, the beliefs of the individual are the highest priority. Postmodern "religion" emphasizes that religious truth is highly individualistic, subjective, and resides within the individual.

Postmodernism seems to mean anything, everything, and nothing. Whatever any individual thinks about something is perfectly okay and correct for that person. Furthermore, since his belief is valid for him, it should not be judged as good or bad by someone else. Everybody's ideas are appropriate and okay, providing they don't harm someone else.

With postmodernism, no position can have any more credibility than any other. All beliefs are equally valid and equally invalid. It is perfectly acceptable for you to believe any set of ideas, as long as you don't impose them on anyone else. Human beings are "whatever we say we are."

Postmodern ideologies are contrary to many Christian beliefs. A major conflict between Christianity and postmodernism is the issue of "absolutes." Postmodernism challenges the notion that, in Scripture, we have absolute truth and only one way to heaven.

For Christians, biblical truth is absolute, objective, knowable, and eternal. The teaching of the Bible is true for everyone, whether they believe it or not. Christianity does not and cannot embrace postmodernism.

We demolish arguments and every pretension that sets itself up against the knowledge of God, and we take captive every thought to make it obedient to Christ. (2 Corinthians 10:5)

All Scripture is God-breathed and is useful for teaching, rebuking, correcting, and training in righteousness, so that the servant of God may be thoroughly equipped for every good work. (2 Tim 3:16.17)

Jesus answered, "I am the way and the truth and the life. No one comes to the Father except through me". (John 14:6)

Your Word is truth. (John 17:17)

Stand firm then, with the belt of truth buckled around your waist. (Ephesians 6:14)

See to it that no one takes you captive through hollow and deceptive philosophy, which depends on human tradition and the elemental spiritual forces of this world rather than on Christ. (Colossians 2:8)

Then you will know the truth, and the truth will set you free. (John 8:32)

 Notes for reflection

God Knows the Future!

God knows the future, according to the Bible. This concept is difficult for us to understand because we humans don't know what the future holds. How can God possibly know what is going to happen before it happens? Nevertheless, biblical prophecy is proof that God knows the future. Biblical prophecies are incredible!

Jesus fulfilled more than 300 prophecies in the Bible. Peter Stoner in Science Speaks (Chicago: Moody Press, 1963) calculated the probability of one man fulfilling 48 prophecies to be one in 10 to the 157th power. That is one chance in 10,000, 000, 000, 000, 000, 000, 000, 000, 000, 000, 000, 000, 000, 000, 000, 000, 000, 000, 000, 000, 000, 000, 000, 000, 000, 000, 000, 000, 000, 000, 000, 000, 000, 000, 000, 000, 000, 000, 000, 000, 000, 000, 000, 000, 000, 000, 000, 000, 000, 000.

These completed prophecies could not have happened by mere chance! Only a supernatural God could have inspired and fulfilled them. The evidence of completed prophecies should convince anyone beyond a reasonable doubt that God knows the future. God has fulfilled these prophecies so that you could "figure out" that He is real and the Bible is true.

Here are some details regarding what God foresees about the future. He knows how many days we each will live. God has our hair numbered. God knows the words on our tongue before we say them. He also knows all of our thoughts, actions, and how everything will end. Miraculously God knows every detail about our future. Prophecies should help us to trust God more because He knows the beginning and the end.

I am telling you before it comes to pass so that when it does occur, you may believe that I am He. (John 13:19, John 14:29)

And even the very hairs of your head are all numbered, so don't be afraid. (Matthew 10:30,31)

For you know when I sit and when I rise; you perceive my thoughts from afar. Even before a word is on my tongue, you, Lord, know it altogether. Your eyes saw my unformed body; all the days ordained for me were written in your book before one of them came to be. (Psalm 139:2,4,16)

Great is our Lord and mighty in power; his understanding has no limit. (Psalm 147:5)

I make known the end from the beginning, from ancient times, what is still to come. I say, "My purpose will stand, and I will do all that I please." (Isaiah 46:10)

Oh, the depth of the riches both of the wisdom and knowledge of God! How unsearchable are his judgments and his ways past finding out? (Romans 11:33)

I am the Alpha and the Omega, the First and the Last, the Beginning and the End. (Revelation 22:13)

 Notes for reflection

What is the Chance?

What is the chance for all the biblical prophecies about Christ's life to be fulfilled? There are over 55 prophecies in the Old Testament, predicting Christ's life and death. When scholars look at these predictions written before Jesus' existence, it is nearly impossible for them to all be true!

Peter Stoner, Chairman of the Departments of Mathematics and Astronomy at Pasadena College, was passionate about biblical prophecies. He calculated that the chance happening for just eight of these prophecies was one chance in 10^{17} possibilities.

Here are just a few of the 55 prophecies written about Christ before his existence:

- Jesus was born of a virgin.
- Like the Passover Lamb, none of Christ's bones would be broken.
- They would cast lots for Jesus' clothing.
- Messiah would be born in Bethlehem.
- Messiah would come from the line of Abraham.
- Messiah would be a descendant of Isaac.
- Messiah would be a descendant of Jacob.
- Messiah would come from the tribe of Judah.
- Messiah's throne will be anointed and eternal.
- Messiah would spend a season in Egypt.
- A massacre of children would happen at Messiah's birthplace.
- A messenger would prepare the way for Messiah.
- Messiah would be declared the Son of God.
- Messiah would be called a Nazarene.
- Messiah would bring light to Galilee.
- Messiah would speak in parables.
- His own people would reject Messiah.

The possible happening of only eight of these predictions in the Old Testament, according to Dr. Stoner, is one chance in 100,000,000,000,000,000. Those are terrible odds for a non-believer to risk life for eternity. Many atheists are betting their eternal lives on a "one out of trillions" chance that biblical predictions are not valid and accurate.

A Timeline for Jesus' Return

What needs to happen on earth before Jesus comes back? Here are some biblical guidelines:

Israel will return to the "Promised Land."
For I will take you out of the nations; I will gather you from all the countries and bring you back into your own land. (Ezekiel 36:24) (Done-1948,1967)

Everyone will hear the Gospel.
And the gospel must first be preached to all nations. (Mark 13:10)

And this gospel of the kingdom will be preached in the whole world as a testimony to all nations, and then the end will come. (Matthew 24:14)

There will be an increase in wars, violence, and lawlessness.
And you will hear of wars and rumors of wars. See that you are not troubled; for all these things must come to pass, but the end is not yet. For nation will rise against nation, and kingdom against kingdom. And because lawlessness will abound, the love of many will grow cold. (Matthew 24:6,7,12)

God said to Noah, "I am going to put an end to all people, for the earth is filled with violence because of them. (Genesis 6:13)

As it was in the days of Noah, so it will be at the coming of the Son of Man. (Matthew 24:37)

There will be earthquakes, famine, pestilence, and catastrophes, such as floods, tornadoes, hurricanes, fires.
Then Jesus said to them: There will be great earthquakes, famines, and pestilences in various places, and fearful events and great signs from heaven. (Luke 21:10,11)

There will be an increase in immorality, lovers of pleasure and money, disobedience to parents, false godliness, scoffing.

143

But know this, that in the last days perilous times will come: For men will be lovers of themselves, lovers of money, boasters, proud, blasphemers, disobedient to parents, unthankful, unholy, unloving, unforgiving, slanderers, without self-control, brutal, despisers of good, traitors, headstrong, haughty, lovers of pleasure rather than lovers of God, having a form of godliness but denying its power. (2 Timothy 3:1–5)

Above all, you must understand that in the last days scoffers will come, scoffing and following their own evil desires. They will say, "Where is this 'coming' he promised? Ever since our ancestors died, everything goes on as it has since the beginning of creation." (2 Peter 3:3,4)

There will be persecution of Christians.

Then they will deliver you up to tribulation and kill you, and you will be hated by all nations for My name's sake" (Matthew 24:9). An increase in Christian persecution. (Mark 13:9-13)

A global world leader will promise peace (an anti-Christ).

This religious leader will possess great charisma and will exercise a powerful influence over political power. (Revelation 13, 17, 19)

This man will have supernatural power to deceive! He will have the ability to perform great miracles, such as causing fire to come down out of the sky. (Revelation 13:13–14)

The Chip

All people, great and small, rich and poor, free and slave, were forced to receive a mark on their right hands or on their foreheads so that they could not buy or sell unless they had the mark, which is the name of the beast or the number of its name. (Revelation 13:16, 17)

Get Adopted Fast!

Once upon a time, a King was very wealthy and owned everything because he made it all. He had total power because he made power. He was totally wise because he made all wisdom. He, amazingly, was loving despite creating and owning everything.

He decided to create people so that he could love them and help them live spectacular lives. The people were to start off being very small, but they would grow up into big people. All were to be help-less, weak, and not so smart. Even worse, they were all just naturally selfish and greedy; they were just born that way.

The King had a plan to give each of the people a spectacular op-portunity to inherit his kingdom. What a deal! He was willing to adopt anyone into his family, but there was a small condition. They each needed to ask the King for two things: ask him for forgiveness for doing selfish things, and secondly, ask the King to be king in their life.

It would be easy to be adopted: there would be no requirements like a financial payment, great strength, or athletic ability needed; no wisdom cut off; no hard work required. Just say "yes" to the King's offer for free forgiveness and the King to be lord of his or her life.

What a fantastic deal! Can you believe it? Agree to those two conditions, and you get the King's kingdom as an inheritance! It is such an easy decision. By the way, If you were one of those little kids, what would you do? GET ADOPTED FAST!

The Spirit you received brought about your adoption to sonship and testifies that we are God's children. Now, if we are children, then we are heirs—heirs of God and co-heirs with Christ that we may also share in his glory. (Romans 8:14-17)

My Father's house has many rooms, and I go to prepare a place for you. I will come back and take you to be with me that you also may be where I am. (John 14:2,3)

If you declare with your mouth, "Jesus is Lord," and believe in your heart that God raised him from the dead, you will be saved. (Romans 10:9,10)

If we confess our sins, he is faithful and just and will forgive us our sins and purify us from all unrighteousness. (1 John 1:9)

For God so loved the world that he gave his one and only Son, that whoever believes in him shall not perish but have eternal life. (John 3:16)

Yet to all who did receive him, to those who believed in his name, he gave the right to become children of God. (John 1:12)

 Notes for reflection

Of Whom is God Most Appreciative?

Who does God really like? Here is what God says: "This is whom I esteem: He who is humble, contrite and trembles at my Word." (Isaiah 66:2)

Three little things to do: that's pretty easy.

1. Be "humble"; don't be proud, arrogant, domineering, bossy, or crabby.
2. Be "contrite"; that is, be sorry for all your sins.
3. "Tremble at God's Word!" What does that mean? Trembling at God's Word is becoming a lost art, but God does think very highly of those who tremble at His Word! Here are a few "tremble verses" to help us.

Lord, do not rebuke me in your anger or discipline me in your wrath. Have mercy on me, Lord, for I am faint. (Psalm 6:1,2)

Consider, therefore, the kindness and sternness of God: sternness to those who fell, but kindness to you, provided that you continue in his kindness. Otherwise, you also will be cut off. (Romans 11:22)

For the Lord, your God is a consuming fire, a jealous God. (Deuteronomy 4:24, Hebrews 12:29)

For we know him who said, "It is mine to avenge; I will repay," and again, "The Lord will judge his people." It is a dreadful thing to fall into the hands of the living God. (Hebrews 10:31)

Whoever believes in the Son has eternal life; whoever does not obey the Son shall not see life, but the wrath of God remains on him. (John 3:36)

For the wrath of God is revealed from heaven against all ungodliness and unrighteousness of men, who by their unrighteousness suppress the truth. (Romans 1:18)

And do not fear those who kill the body but cannot kill the soul. Rather fear him who can destroy both soul and body in hell. (Matthew 10:28)

For if we go on sinning deliberately after receiving the knowledge of the truth, there no longer remains a sacrifice for sins, but a fearful expectation of judgment. It is a fearful thing to fall into the hands of the living God. (Hebrews 10:26-31)

 **Notes for reflection**

You Lost Everything!

Imagine that you have just lost everything; all your money, possessions, family, and health! Everything is gone, and all you have left is Jesus! How would you do?

It sounds like a disaster, just you and Jesus. But actually, let's examine that a bit more. It is true, all of your earthly possessions may be gone, but we humans underestimate the supreme value of being with Jesus.

Let's start with the Beatitudes:

- You inherit the entire kingdom of God because you are humble and poor in spirit.
- You are blessed and comforted by God because you mourn.
- You are blessed and "filled" as you hunger and thirst for God.
- You inherit the entire planet earth because you are now meek. Wow!
- You see God because you have been pure of heart.
- You are a Child of God because you have been a peacemaker on earth.
- Let's end with the fact that Jesus has given you God's Glory!

I, Jesus, have given them the glory that you gave me, that they may be one as we are one. (John 17:22)

Even If you have lost everything, Jesus will greatly bless you as well as provide for you. To be honest, what the Lord has for you is much more than you can imagine!

Blessed are the poor in spirit, for theirs is the kingdom of heaven.
Blessed are those who mourn, for they will be comforted.
Blessed are the meek, for they will inherit the earth.
Blessed are those who hunger and thirst for righteousness, for they will be filled.
Blessed are the merciful, for they will be shown mercy.

Blessed are the pure in heart, for they will see God.

Blessed are the peacemakers, for they will be called children of God.

Blessed are those who are persecuted because of righteousness, for theirs is the kingdom of heaven.

Blessed are you when people insult you, persecute you and falsely say all kinds of evil against you because of me. Rejoice and be glad, because great is your reward in heaven. (Matthew 5:3-12)

You will fill me with joy in your presence, with eternal pleasures at your right hand. (Psalm 16:11)

 Notes for reflection

Locked-in Syndrome

Locked-In Syndrome is a terrible, dreaded stroke in the brain, leaving patients completely alert but without any physical strength. It can be so complete that patients can only move their eyelids to signify "yes" or "no."

What possible value is life if all you could do is move your eyelids? Eating would be impossible, and sitting in a wheelchair would be nearly impossible. What possible value would there be to keep a "Locked-in Syndrome" patient alive?

VERY MUCH! These patients can hear and see and think; they know that life itself is very precious. Even though they cannot move, they have an incredible opportunity to draw near to God. The good news is that many of the distractions we experience preventing closeness to God are forever gone.

Most importantly, these patients can pray, and their prayers can unleash tremendous power. Today, remember the benefits of Locked-In Syndrome and appreciate not having that disease. Thank the Lord for your good health and fight ugly distractions keeping you from God. Don't forget that your prayer life may be your most valuable possession!

For the Lord your God is living among you. He is a mighty savior. He will take delight in you with gladness. With his love, he will calm all your fears. He will rejoice over you with joyful songs. (Zephaniah 3:17)

Love the Lord your God with all your heart and with all your soul and with all your strength and with all your mind. (Luke 10:27)

The prayer of a righteous person is powerful and effective. (James 5:16)

And we know that in all things, God works for the good of those who love him, who have been called according to his purpose. (Romans 8:28)

For I am convinced that neither death nor life, neither angels nor demons, neither the present nor the future, nor any powers, neither height nor depth, nor anything else in all creation, will be able to separate us from the love of God that is in Christ Jesus our Lord. (Romans 8:38,39)

 Notes for reflection

Pick Your Favorite Relationship with the Lord

We humans have many "relationships with the Lord" from which to choose. Which of the following four options do you prefer, and in which do you spend the most time?

1. Slave
2. Servant
3. Child of God
4. Bride of Christ

To be a slave sounds terrible! The nations of the world have been trying to end slavery for many years. Slavery has been a terrible scourge in the past. On the other hand, being a slave to the Lord may have some excellent benefits. I know this concept is a stretch for most of us to consider, but let me give it a try.

A friend of mine signed her letters with "Bondslave of Jesus Christ" placed under her signature. She had an excellent reason for doing that; it gave her many opportunities to explain her loving personal relationship with the Lord.

Here are some benefits of becoming a slave of the Lord.

#1 You are His property, and He is responsible for everything. Therefore, your problems are His problems, and He helps you deal with what you cannot handle.

#2 He makes many of your decisions; what to do, where to live, what job you should take. Don't you get tired of making all your own decisions? Why not have the Lord, who is "all-wise," "all-loving," and "all-powerful," make your big decisions? He will do a much better job than you could do.

#3 He is your physician, miracle worker, travel agent, grocery store, financier, and so much more.

Be a slave to God; it's the best relationship during a very severe storm. He will take great care of you because you are "His property"! Give all your fear and anxiety to Him; enjoy the "freedom of being His slave"!

Live as free people, but do not use your freedom as a cover-up for evil; live as God's slaves. (1 Peter 2:16)

But now that you have been set free from sin and have become slaves of God, the benefit you reap leads to holiness, and the result is eternal life. (Romans 6:22)

Though I am free and belong to no one, I have made myself a slave to everyone, to win as many as possible. (1 Corinthians 9:19)

Obey them not only to win their favor when their eye is on you but as slaves of Christ, doing the will of God from your heart. (Ephesians 6:6)

 **Notes for reflection**

Personal Relationship with God

Humans have choices for our relationship with the Lord: If being the Lord's slave doesn't fit your preference, what do you think about becoming His servant? A servant has more options or benefits than a slave has. A servant, for one thing, can just quit if work gets too challenging. If Jesus is your boss, however, why would you ever want to leave?

Sometimes I feel too tired to do what I know God wants me to do. At those moments, I find it best to become God's "servant." Maybe I can bargain to get a break. However, most times, I have no decision in the matter. It's good that I like my boss, and when it's all done, I'm happier doing what He asks me to do whenever He tells me to do it.

In our culture, being a servant is a somewhat lowly task. That is not true if you are a servant to the Lord. Rejoice in being a servant to Almighty God; take great pride and be worthy of your high position! Enjoy doing what your boss says; He will take excellent care of you. After these verses, you may want to become the Lord's servant more often.

This, then, is how you ought to regard us: as servants of Christ and as those entrusted with the mysteries God has revealed. (1 Corinthians 4:1)

All Scripture is God-breathed and is useful for teaching, rebuking, correcting, and training in righteousness, so that the servant of God may be thoroughly equipped for every good work. (2 Timothy 3:16,17)

Sitting down, Jesus called the Twelve and said, "Anyone who wants to be first must be the very last, and the servant of all." (Mark 9:35)

The greatest among you will be your servant. (Matthew 23:11)

Then a voice came from the throne, saying: "Praise our God, all you servants, you who fear him, both great and small!" (Revelation 19:5)

The Favored "Child of God" Relationship

Here is the most comfortable relationship with Jesus and the most favored role for many of us; the "Child of God" relationship. Praise the Lord for this one. Whew! We adults easily understand this role; it's so easy to become a child. Life can be so tricky with many problems challenging us; nothing could be better than this "little child" position. Laughing, splashing, playing all day; there's not much work to do. The days are long, the sun is bright, and life is fantastic!

Even though you are an adult, frequently in your imagination, try becoming a little child and go on a walk holding the Lord's hand. Have you ever been able to crawl up onto the lap of Jesus in your imagination? Enjoy going to sleep with "our Father who art in heaven" tenderly watching over you. Enjoy being a child of God!

The Lord desires us to be His children. The stress is limited, and there should be no anxiety. It's a great promotion. The Bible says we need to become like little children with childlike faith and trust!

And Jesus said, "Truly I tell you, unless you change and become like little children, you will never enter the kingdom of heaven." (Matthew 18:3)

Therefore, whoever takes the lowly position of this child is the greatest in the kingdom of heaven. And whoever welcomes one such child in my name welcomes me. (Matthew 18:4,5)

Jesus said, "Let the little children come to me, and do not hinder them, for the kingdom of heaven belongs to such as these." (Matthew 19:14)

Truly I tell you, anyone who will not receive the kingdom of God as a little child will never enter it. (Mark 10:15)

Those who are led by the Spirit of God are the children of God. (Romans 8:14)

So in Christ Jesus, you are all children of God through faith. (Galatians 3:26)

Yet to all who did receive him, to those who believed in His name, he gave the right to become children of God. (John 1:12)

See what great love the Father has lavished on us, that we should be called children of God! And that is what we are! (1 John 3:1)

 Notes for reflection

Sons of God

Okay, many of you are struggling with becoming a "little child" with God. If you prefer to switch from a "child" to "sonship," that is also correct. Being a "son of God" might mean more responsibility, though, depending upon just how old a son you are. No matter what, you still qualify as a child of God, just an older one.

Here are some verses if you prefer to grow up into "sonship."

The Spirit you received brought about your adoption to sonship. (Romans 8:15)

He predestined us to adoption as sons through Jesus Christ to Himself, according to the kind intention of His will. (Ephesians 1:5)

Because you are his sons, God sent the Spirit of His Son into our hearts, the Spirit who calls out, "Abba, Father." (Galatians 4:6)

 Notes for reflection

Relationship: The Bride of Christ

We, the church, are to be the "bride of Christ." What does that mean? It's beautiful, I am sure, but a bit intimidating also. Lord, forgive us for our lack of understanding in this sensitive area and let us prepare well. Let's explore some of the issues.

First, being the bride of Christ is God's idea. It is amazing, humbling, and beyond our imagination. Some theologians conjecture that there have been around four billion "followers of God" since the beginning of time. There is comfort in numbers with so many of us; one could blend in and often go unnoticed. It seems pretty safe to be somewhere in the middle of four billion people who are the bride of Christ.

But what if it's just me being the bride of Christ? Just me? Alone? From Jesus' standpoint, to have me as His bride would be a quantum leap considering my sinfulness. It would be very, very special, but still a bit intimidating and incredible.

At present, God is preparing the church to become the bride of Christ, but it seems that we are not there yet. Scripture talks about our future marriage supper as a sumptuous feast of celebration. That day will come, but at present, it is beyond our imagination. We know It will be glorious and spectacular. The very reason Jesus left Heaven and died for us is that we, the church, will become the bride of Christ. So let us prepare and look forward to our big day!

Husbands, love your wives, even as Christ also loved the church, and gave himself for it; that he might present it to himself a glorious church, not having spot, or wrinkle, or any such thing; but that it should be holy and without blemish. (Ephesians 5:25-27)

As a young man marries a young woman, so will your Builder marry you; as a bridegroom rejoices over his bride, so will your God rejoice over you. (Isaiah 62:5)

For this reason, a man will leave his father and mother and be united to his wife, and the two will become one flesh. This is a profound mystery—but I am talking about Christ and the church. (Ephesians 5:31,32)

I am jealous for you with a godly jealousy. I promised you to one husband, to Christ, so that I might present you as a pure virgin to him. (2 Corinthians 11:2)

Let us rejoice and be glad and give him glory! For the wedding of the Lamb has come, and his bride has made herself ready. I saw the Holy City, the new Jerusalem, coming down out of heaven from God, prepared as a bride beautifully dressed for her husband. (Revelation 19:7, 21:2)

 Notes for reflection

There are no "Singles" in Heaven

It might upset some and thrill others that singleness is not allowed in heaven; we all will be married to Jesus Christ. It all started when we accepted Jesus as Lord and Savior. In God's perfect timing, there will be a "swoosh" when we die and go to Heaven.

After getting to Heaven, we, the church, will be invited to the grand marriage celebration that Jesus has planned. Believe it or not, His marriage to the church is the reason Jesus came to earth. We, the church, become Christ's bride; we actually get married to Christ. Wow! That event is so much beyond our comprehension!

Prepare for this most glorious, "out of this world" experience! It seems too good to be true and is so beyond our imagination. Nevertheless, each of us might be a bit edgy; there's a smidgen of caution and concern. We might feel a bit out of control, understanding that significant changes are coming. How are you doing right now? Are you feeling uneasy?

A good solution would be to recall the close times you have experienced with Jesus during your lifetime. Here is a suggested prayer for you to pray: "Thank you, Jesus, for teaching me about yourself in the Bible. Thank you for the close fellowship we have shared in times of prayer. Thank you for the love and care that you have shown me during my difficult times. I look forward with faith, hope, and love to being your bride!"

For the husband is the head of the wife as Christ is the head of the church, his body, of which He is the Savior. (Ephesians 5:23)

Then the angel said to me, "Blessed are those who are invited to the wedding supper of the Lamb!" And he added, "These are the true words of God." (Revelation 19:9)

I saw the Holy City, the new Jerusalem, coming down out of heaven from God, prepared as a bride beautifully dressed for her husband. Come, I will show you the bride, the wife of the Lamb. (Revelation 21:2,9)

My Father's house has many rooms; I (Jesus) am going there to prepare a place for you. And if I go and prepare a place for you, I will come back and take you to be with me that you also may be where I am. (John 14:2,3)

And now these three remain: faith, hope, and love. But the greatest of these is love. (1 Corinthians 13:13)

It is written: "What no eye has seen, what no ear has heard, and what no human mind has conceived—the things God has prepared for those who love him." (1 Corinthians 2:9)

 Notes for reflection

Is God in Control of our Problems?

Is God in control of our problems? For the Christian, difficulties in our lives may have significant value, but do these problems come from God? This big question raises two possibilities; which do you think is right?

1. Bad things that happen to us are simply unfortunate chance happenings?
2. Bad things that happen to us are allowed by a loving God to benefit us spiritually?

Here is a scriptural defense suggesting that problems are allowed into our lives by a loving God who means them for our good! After reading them, it is up to you to decide if God has used problems in your life for your good so far. Don't forget that the Lord has eternity to show you the benefits of your pain and difficulties.

All things work together for good to those who love the Lord and are called according to His purpose. (Romans 8:28)

For our light and momentary troubles are achieving for us an eternal glory that far outweighs them all. (2 Corinthians 4:17)

You intended to harm me, but God intended it for good to accomplish what is now being done, the saving of many lives. (Genesis 50:20)

Consider it pure joy, my brothers and sisters, whenever you face trials of many kinds because you know that the testing of your faith produces perseverance. Let perseverance finish its work so that you may be mature and complete, not lacking anything. (James 1:2-4)

It was good for me to be afflicted so that I might learn your decrees. (Psalm 119:71)

"For my thoughts are not your thoughts; neither are your ways my ways," declares the Lord. "As the heavens are higher than the earth, so are my ways higher than your ways and my thoughts than your thoughts." (Isaiah 55:8,9)

I form the light and create darkness, I bring prosperity and create disaster; I, the Lord, do all these things. (Isaiah 45:7)

He who did not spare his own Son but gave him up for us all—how will he not also, along with him, graciously give us all things? (Romans 8:32)

We also glory in our sufferings because we know that suffering produces perseverance; perseverance, character; and character, hope. (Romans 5:3,4)

 Notes for reflection

Turning Pain into Great Value

How can anyone turn pain into something valuable? I don't like pain; it hurts. Nobody likes pain; even the fear of pain is painful. Physical, emotional, and mental pain are all pain, and each one hurts.

Is it possible to turn painful experiences into something valuable? If we could, it might at least give pain some meaning and purpose. Sooner or later, we all will suffer heartbreaking tragedy. You might be surprised that there is any benefit to pain. It is good to look forward to that benefit!

Here's the "faith" challenge; first, realize that the Lord desires that your troubles "achieve for you an eternal glory that far outweighs the pain." Next, pray that your pain will have purpose and meaning; pray that it will miraculously achieve for you a tremendous eternal blessing beyond your imagination!

For our light and momentary troubles are achieving for us an eternal glory that far outweighs them all. (2 Corinthians 4:17)

And we know that for those who love God, all things work together for good, for those who are called according to His purpose. (Romans 8:28)

Count it pure joy, my brothers and sisters, when you face trials of many kinds because you know that the testing of your faith produces perseverance, so you may be mature and complete, not lacking anything. (James 1:2-4)

Therefore, in order to keep me from becoming conceited, I was given a thorn in my flesh, a messenger of Satan, to torment me. Three times I pleaded with the Lord to take it away from me. But he said to me, "My grace is sufficient for you, for my power is made perfect in weakness.

Therefore I will boast all the more gladly about my weaknesses, so that Christ's power may rest on me." (2 Corinthians 12:7-9)

But those who suffer, He delivers in their suffering; He speaks to them in their affliction. (Job 36:15)

The Lord is close to the brokenhearted; he rescues those whose spirits are crushed. (Psalm 34:18)

He comforts us in all our troubles so that we can comfort others. When they are troubled, we will be able to give them the same comfort God has given us. (2 Corinthians 1:4)

Even though I walk through the darkest valley, I will fear no evil, for you are with me. (Psalm 23:4)

 Notes for reflection

The Most Disgusting Place in all God's Creation

What's the most disgusting place in all God's creation? With trillions and trillions of galaxies, black holes, bubbling sulfur, animal stuff, etc., give it your best guess to describe the most awful, disgusting place in all of God's creation.

Would it be here on planet earth or some huge hot swamp somewhere out in space? Wherever you imagine it, now claim that area to be under the Lordship of Jesus Christ. After all, He made it for His glory, even if it's disgusting. He is sovereign and in control of it.

When you experience something disgusting, is there some reason that God made it? Try this exercise: attempt to enjoy the awful smell of a skunk when passing roadkill. That terrible smell makes clean air even more lovely! Somehow enjoy miserably hot summer days for what they are. Enjoy freezing cold days for the same reason. God made them both, and each say something about God's creativity.

This thought is a bit of a stretch, but maybe the worst place in all creation is where your enemies are. For sure, that would be a disgusting place to be right now. How can we cover that place with the Lordship of Jesus Christ and have God glorify Himself there?

Here is what Jesus suggests: "Love your enemies, do good to them, and lend to them without expecting to get anything back. Then your reward will be great, and you will be children of the Most High. Be merciful, just as your Father is merciful." (Luke 6:35,36) Being with your enemies is a pretty disgusting place, but if you offer your forgiveness to them, the situation has the possibility for great reward despite the awful stink!

Here is another verse that tells us that God will be with us in disgusting places: "Yea, though I walk through the valley of the shadow of death, I will fear no evil, for You are with me; Your rod and staff, they comfort me. You prepare a table before me in the presence of my enemies." (Psalm 23:4,5)

Keep alert for disgusting places. They may help you love God more and even provide you with a great reward.

One God and Father of all, who is over all, through all, and in all. (Ephesians 4:6)

God saw all that he had made, and it was very good. (Genesis 1:31)

Skunk spray is made up of sulfur compounds, causing headaches, burning, or stinging in the eyes. A skunk can spray six strikes, which can each travel 10 feet. The aromatic spray will send even a large bear running in the opposite direction. God made skunks!

 **Notes for reflection**

The Faith Chamber

How are you doing in your "Faith Chamber"? It's the frightening place where we occasionally find ourselves when we seriously need God's miraculous help. Noah's faith chamber probably lasted for years while he built the Ark. King David's faith chamber with Goliath probably took only minutes. Some people have many faith chambers during their lifetime; King David had many.

Faith chambers are designed to grow faith. When you find yourself in your faith chamber, don't get too discouraged; God is there with you. He desires these chambers to be a special time to get to know Him better, pray like never before, and experience His miraculous power. Fill your faith chamber with as much faith and trust as you can muster; the more, the better! He won't keep you there beyond what you can handle.

When the Lord answers your prayer and shows you how to get out, you will be so relieved and thankful. Your faith and trust will be stronger should you step into a more frightening chamber in the future.

Are you presently in a challenging faith chamber? Your faith chamber is different from everyone else's, but God is there with you. Here are some verses to help while you are in the crucible.

No temptation has overtaken you, except what is common to mankind. And God is faithful; he will not let you be tempted beyond what you can bear. But when you are tempted, he will also provide a way out so that you can endure it. (1 Corinthians 10:13)

Ask, and it will be given to you; seek, and you will find; knock, and the door will be opened to you. For everyone who asks receives; the one who seeks finds; and to the one who knocks, the door will be opened. (Matthew 7:7)

I can do all things through him who gives me strength. (Philippians 4:13)

And we know that in all things, God works for the good of those who love Him, who have been called according to His purpose. (Romans 8:28)

Without faith, it is impossible to please God. (Hebrews 11:6)

Truly, I tell you, if you have faith as small as a mustard seed, you can say to this mountain, "Move from here to there," and it will move. Nothing will be impossible for you. (Matthew 17:20)

My grace is sufficient for you, for my power is made perfect in weakness. (2 Corinthians 12:9)

I pray that the eyes of your heart may be enlightened in order that you may know that incomparable power available to you. That power is the same as the mighty strength He exerted when He raised Christ from the dead. (Ephesians 1:18-20)

Notes for reflection

Punda wa Jesu

"Punda wa Jesu" means "donkey for Jesus" in Swahili. A recent graduate from an African seminary felt that God had called him to be a "donkey for Jesus." He knew that he would need to walk long distances to lead Bible studies or preach. He would be carrying lots of things and helping other people along the way. It meant that he should be obedient like a donkey even though they do bray (complain) and kick at times. His destiny was to work hard for Jesus.

I would do well to rise to the "high calling" of being a punda wa Jesu (donkey for Jesus) in my life. The problem is, however, that it's challenging to carry other people's burdens. I notice that when I try to be a donkey, I kick and bray instead of pray. Nevertheless, becoming a donkey for Jesus may be the most important goal that I could pursue in my activities with other people. Would you care to join me, now and then, and become a donkey for Jesus?

Do not think of yourself more highly than you ought, but rather think of yourself with sober judgment, in accordance with the faith God has distributed to each of you. (Romans 12:3)

And what does the Lord require of you? To act justly and to love mercy and to walk humbly with your God. (Micah 6:8)

Whoever wants to become great among you must be your servant, and whoever wants to be first must be your slave—just as the Son of Man did not come to be served, but to serve, and to give his life as a ransom for many. (Matthew 20:26-28)

Then Jesus said to his disciples, "Whoever wants to be my disciple must deny themselves and take up their cross and follow me." (Matthew 16:24, Mark 8:34, Luke 9:23)

How Small are you Compared to God?

Atheists believe that God does not exist. Non-Christians feel that God is not important. When a person becomes a Christian, God becomes very important. However, often the new Christian doesn't recognize God's incredible power and significance. The new Christian may need to increase His knowledge of who God is.

Early in my Christian journey, I promised to give the Lord five minutes each day of my valuable time. I thought that was a pretty good deal for the Lord and a big sacrifice on my part. Later, as God became more important to me, I committed more time to prayer and the Bible each day.

As Christians grow deeper in the Lord, their own importance gets smaller compared to God's significance. A worthy goal is to "magnify" the Lord; that is, make Him bigger and bigger. The bigger God gets, the smaller we become in comparison. How small are you compared to God?

There is value in being small and weak in our eyes because our weaknesses may allow God's power to be made perfect in us. The Lord told St. Paul that His strength is made perfect in Paul's weakness.

Magnify God so that He gets tremendous; then, in comparison, you will get smaller. Your smallness and weakness may result in God's power being available to you in ways beyond what you can imagine. Your weakness allows God's power to be unleashed in you. How are you doing, making God really big and yourself small compared to Him?

But he said to me, "My grace is sufficient for you, for my power is made perfect in weakness." Therefore, I will boast all the more gladly about my weaknesses so that Christ's power may rest on me. That is why, for Christ's sake, I delight in weaknesses, in insults, in hardships, in persecutions, in difficulties. For when I am weak, then I am strong. (2 Corinthians 12:9,10)

Blessed are the poor in spirit (those who see themselves as weak and very dependent on God), for theirs is the kingdom of heaven. (Matthew 5:3)

God resists the proud but gives grace to the humble. (James 4:6)

Humble yourselves in the sight of the Lord, and He will lift you up. (James 4:10)

My flesh and my heart may fail, but God is the strength of my heart and my portion forever. (Psalm 73:26)

Gideon's story shows us that when God wants to use us, he often begins by weakening us. (Judges 7:7)

 Notes for reflection

The Fear of God

The "fear of God" is an unusual and even slightly taboo topic these days. We much prefer to focus on God's love, grace, and compassion, rather than a God to be feared. Historically, however, the fear of God was healthy; fear kept many people from engaging in malicious or immoral activities because they feared His punishment.

Currently, our society is redefining "immoral activities" into being "okay activities." What was acknowledged as sin in the past is now accepted as normal. Many enjoy this new freedom of living without "right" and "wrong." Wisdom tells us that sooner or later, disaster will result.

Your "fear of God" will serve you well during your lifetime. It is vital for your spiritual health! Here is a Scriptural starting place to encourage your "fear of God."

Moses said to the people, "Do not be afraid. God has come to test you; the fear of God will be with you to keep you from sinning." (Exodus 20:20)

So, worship God acceptably with reverence and awe, for our "God is a consuming fire." (Hebrews 12:29)

These are the ones I look on with favor: those who are humble and contrite in spirit and who tremble at my word. (Isaiah 66:2)

Woe to those who call evil good and good evil, who put darkness for light and light for darkness. (Isaiah 5:20)

He said in a loud voice, "Fear God and give Him glory because the hour of his judgment has come." (Revelation 14:7)

Show proper respect to everyone, love the family of believers, fear God. (1 Peter 2:17)

God's Boot

I have been trying to keep ahead of God's boot. It can be painful. God's boot is a loving correction that works for my good. The boot is a good thing even though it may sting a bit, sometimes a lot! God's love is always involved, even if mixed with some pain.

Generally, God uses the boot when I stray where I shouldn't be going in the first place. It "pops" me back onto the path. Some folks have strayed so far from God's way that He stops using His boot on them. Don't go down that path.

Here is a description of the different types of boots that He sometimes uses: speeding tickets, pain, sickness, car accidents, hard times. What are the loving boot bumps that you have experienced in the past? Any right now?

The smack of God's boot should draw us closer to God and make us love Him more and more. When we get to heaven, we may delight in touching, hugging, and even kissing God's different boots that He has used on us. We will be forever grateful for each loving thump they gave us!

My son, do not make light of the Lord's discipline and do not lose heart when he rebukes you because the Lord disciplines the one he loves, and he chastens everyone he accepts as his son. God disciplines us for our good so that we may share in his holiness. No discipline seems pleasant at the time but painful. Later on, however, it produces a harvest of righteousness and peace for those who have been trained by it. (Hebrews 12:6,7,10,11}

We know that in all things, God works for the good of those who love him, who have been called according to his purpose. (Romans 8:28)

Blessed is the one whom God corrects; so do not despise the discipline of the Almighty. (Job 5:17)

Know then in your heart that as a man disciplines his son, so the Lord your God disciplines you. (Deuteronomy 8:5)

You intended to harm me, but God intended it for good to accomplish what is now being done, the saving of many lives. (Genesis 50:20) (Joseph talking to his brothers who sold him into slavery)

 **Notes for reflection**

The Five Percent

I am in the five percent group regarding "pain" theology. In which group are you? I was in a lot of pain and almost died from an unusual condition during my forty-five-day stay at a Mayo Clinic hospital. Here's my theological question: Was this pain and suffering from God, Satan, or just an unfortunate random happening?

Eighty-five percent of Christians would say it is a random happening; the "rain falls on the just and the unjust." Chance difficulties are happening naturally to each of us. That's just life!

Ten percent of Christians would say Satan is to blame. He is like a lion looking for whom he can devour, and sometimes he bites us. After all, Satan comes to steal, kill, and destroy. We live in a fallen world, and pain is from Satan.

Five percent of Christians believe that suffering comes from a very loving Father who desires us to grow deeper and more mature. Pain and suffering are powerful tools to help us reach spiritual heights, not possible in any other way.

As Christians, we are trying to walk as closely as possible with God. If we are forgiven and sold out to Him as Lord of our life, we are in a very safe place. It's safe because God controls the testing, and He will protect us from anything that is not in His permissive will for us.

The "five percent of Christians" believe that our loving God not only "allows" problems but also "sends" them into our lives for our eternal good. God may be testing us or growing us spiritually for His eternal glory. He desires that our suffering results in benefits for us and also that He will be glorified.

There is a plan. Sometimes it is testing us to grow spiritually. It is not by chance. I believe God puts a mighty barrier between us and "chance" happenings. Supernaturally, God can work our difficulties into our good and His glory!

One God and Father of all, who is over all, and through all, and in all. (Ephesians 4:6)

And we know that in all things, God works for the good of those who love him, who have been called according to his purpose. (Romans 8:28)

For our light and momentary troubles are achieving for us an eternal glory that far outweighs them all. (2 Corinthians 4:17)

The Lord, your God, is testing you to find out whether you love him with all your heart and with all your soul. (Deuteronomy 13:3)

I have tested you in the furnace of affliction. (Isaiah 48:10)

And after you have suffered for a little while, the God of all grace will himself restore, support, strengthen, and establish you. (1 Peter 5:10)

Consider it pure joy, my brothers and sisters, whenever you face trials of many kinds because you know that the testing of your faith produces perseverance. Let perseverance finish its work so that you may be mature and complete, not lacking anything. (James 1:2-4)

No temptation has overtaken you, except what is common to humankind. And God is faithful; he will not let you be tempted beyond what you can bear. But when you are tempted, he will also provide a way out so that you can endure it. (1 Corinthians 10:13)

I form light and create darkness. I make well-being and create calamity. I am the Lord, who does all these things. (Isaiah 45:7)

Worse Before it gets Better!

It may get worse before it gets better. That's a depressing thought, but it seems the Bible warns us that we should prepare for the world to get worse. No matter what happens, keep close to God, and surround yourself with good Christian friends for support. Hang in there!

What's wrong with a little bit of pain for planet earth and its people if our heavenly future is OUT OF THIS WORLD! Again, it will get better; much, much better. Put your trust in God; He is sovereign and in control. All things are moving along just according to His plan.

We know that the whole creation has been groaning in labor pains until now; and not only the creation but we ourselves, who have the firstfruits of the Spirit, groan inwardly while we wait for adoption, the redemption of our bodies. (Romans 8:22,23)

On the earth, nations will be in anguish and perplexity at the roaring and tossing of the sea. People will faint from terror, apprehensive of what is coming on the world. (Luke 21:25,26)

Nation will rise against nation, and kingdom against kingdom. There will be famines and earthquakes in various places. Because of the increase of wickedness, the love of most will grow cold. (Matthew 24:6,7,12)

Set your mind on things above, not on earthly things, for your life is now hidden with Christ in God. When Christ, who is your life, appears, then you also will appear with him in glory. (Colossians 3:2-4)

Consider it pure joy, my brothers and sisters, whenever you face trials of many kinds (James 1:2)

Be joyful in hope, patient in affliction, faithful in prayer. (Romans 12:12)

Rejoice in that day and leap for joy because great is your reward in heaven. (Luke 6:23)

You believe in him and are filled with an inexpressible and glorious joy, for you are receiving the end result of your faith, the salvation of your souls. (1 Peter 1:8,9)

For the kingdom of God is righteousness, peace, and joy in the Holy Spirit. (Romans 14:17)

Heaven and earth will pass away, but my words will never pass away. (Luke 21:33)

What no eye has seen, what no ear has heard, and what no human mind has conceived—the things God has prepared for those who love him. (1 Corinthians 2:9)

 Notes for reflection

My Most Difficult Verse!

For me, this verse is the most challenging in the entire Bible. Job was going through terrible difficulties. Painful sores riddled his body; his children were dying, his sheep, goats, and camels were stolen, even his so-called "friends" mocked him. Despite all this tragedy, Job was still able to make this bold statement: "Though he (God) slay me, yet will I hope in him." (Job 13:15)

This incredible challenge could happen to you or me; hopefully not! But if everything goes wrong, would I be able to pray: "Though You, God, allow this disaster to destroy me, I will still trust in You." What a challenge! Pray that it will never, ever happen!

"Everybody has a price," some people say. What is my or your "price" before we would turn away from God? Some folks lose their belief in God for such a small price. Faith is far too precious to abandon for some little reason. Don't go there! Guard your faith so that no tragedy, however big or small, can cause you to lose it.

Jesus knew this verse and was faithful to His death on the cross. Here is my prayer for you and me: Dear Lord, please don't test us this severely. But if it is in your plan, please give us the strength to be faithful. Help us to trust in you no matter what happens! Give us your strength to say loudly and clearly, "Though you slay me, Lord, I will still trust in You!"

Though he (God) slay me, yet will I hope in him! (Job 13:15)

He then began to teach them that the Son of Man must suffer and be killed, and after three days rise again. He spoke plainly about this. (Mark 8:31,32)

About three in the afternoon, Jesus cried out in a loud voice, "Eloi, Eloi, lema sabachtani?" which means, "My God, My God, why have you forsaken me?" (Matthew 27:46, Mark 15:34, Psalm 22:1)

Then he said to them all: "Whoever wants to be my disciple must deny themselves and take up their cross daily and follow me. For whoever wants to save their life will lose it, but whoever loses their life for me will save it." (Luke 9:23,24)

 Notes for reflection

The Dark Zone

The most challenging time in your life may become the most rewarding time when you look back at it. Crisis times are difficult and unbearable; they are scary and feel terribly long. Praying is difficult or almost impossible; doubts arise, and it's a fierce spiritual battle. There should be a name for those times like "the Dark Zone."

When in the terrible "dark zone," your prayers might be the most intense and powerful. You try to be courageous and pray for more faith. The good news is that when in a crisis, the smallest amount of faith that you can muster may be far more powerful than you imagine.

It's pretty easy to pray when everything is going smoothly, but if you can muster even a tiny amount of faith in the dark zone, it has incredible power. When in your dark zone, squeeze out some thankfulness even though you don't feel thankful. Your dark zone faith is being tested by fire, but you will be grateful when it turns into pure gold.

Even more importantly, that terrible dark zone might be the time that Jesus may appreciate the very most! Our helplessness and total dependency may be a very pleasing time to the Lord. He deserves our best attention, and He gets it during our dark zone times.

Keep the Faith as Job did. After it was all over, the Lord doubled his possessions. Don't give up. Fight the battle of faith!

Be strong and courageous. Do not be afraid; do not be discouraged; for the Lord, your God will be with you wherever you go. (Joshua 1:9)

God is our refuge and strength; a very present help in trouble. Therefore, we will not fear. (Psalm 46:1)

Because he loves me, says the Lord, I will rescue him; I will protect him, for he acknowledges my name. He will call on me, and I will answer him; I will be with him in trouble, I will deliver him and honor him. With a long life, I will satisfy him and show him my salvation. (Psalm 91:14-16 The Soldier's Psalm for going into battle)

I will do whatever you ask in my name so that the Father may be glorified in the Son. You may ask me for anything in my name, and I will do it. (John 14:13,14)

The Lord blessed the latter part of Job's life more than the former part. He had fourteen thousand sheep, six thousand camels, a thousand yoke of oxen, and a thousand donkeys. (Job 42:12)

 Notes for reflection

Union with Christ

There are two aspects to our "union with Christ"; one is "Christ in me," and the other is "I in Christ." St. Paul mentioned "in Christ" over 250 times. What does Scripture say about our actually being inside of Christ, and what does "in Christ" even mean?

It could mean that we have the same mindset as Christ has; that is, we think as Jesus thinks. Or it could mean being in Christ's spiritual body. Many theologians believe that it is both; we have the mindset of Christ, but also supernaturally we are in Christ. Either way, it is a beautiful union.

This world has many dangers, and Satan is prowling around looking for who he can devour. Without a doubt, the safest place in this world would be "in Christ." Don't take being "in Christ" for granted. No matter what happens, Jesus Christ loves us, died for us, and wins in the end!

Enjoy the following Scripture and solidify your esteemed position of being "in Christ."

I consider everything a loss that I may gain Christ and be found in him. (Philippians 3:8a,9a)

I am the vine; you are the branches. If you remain in me and I in you, you will bear much fruit; apart from me, you can do nothing. If you remain in me and my words remain in you, ask whatever you wish, and it will be done for you. (John 15:5,7)

Whoever eats my flesh and drinks my blood remains in me, and I in them. (John 6:56)

For as in Adam all die, so in Christ, all will be made alive. (1 Corinthians 15:22

There is neither Jew nor gentile, neither slave nor free, nor is the male or female, for you are all one in Christ Jesus. (Galatians 3:2)

For the Lord himself will come down from heaven, with a loud command, and the dead in Christ will rise first. (1 Thessalonians 4:16)

Therefore, if anyone is in Christ, he is a new creation; the old has gone, the new is here! (2 Corinthians 5:17)

For we are God's handiwork, created in Christ Jesus to do good works, which God prepared in advance for us to do. (Ephesians 2:10)

 Notes for reflection

Christ in Me

What does "Union with God" mean? "Union" is the most exciting topic in this book! The marriage union is our primary example in Scripture; a husband and wife living together. Marriage implies closeness and partnership that has many dimensions.

Our "union with Christ," however, seems to go even further than marriage! Here is a brief picture of the path to union many Christians have experienced. Initially, when we become a follower of Jesus, we visualize Him in heaven and pray to Him there. Later, Jesus comes closer as our friend during devotions once a day. Later in our faith journey, we invite Him to walk with us through our entire day, especially when we go through difficult times.

Next comes the fantastic "union" relationship; we invite Jesus inside of us! Initially, some might feel that He is too close; He is invading our private space. After all, if Christ lives in me, He hears my thoughts, sees what my eyes see, and hears what I hear.

That is all true, but the benefits of "Christ in me" far outweigh those concerns. Devotions are great because He speaks while we read Scripture. "Christ in me" during terribly difficult times is a great comfort. Going into surgery is much better, with Christ living in me.

Take great comfort having the Creator of the Universe not only with you but powerfully in you! If Jesus seems far away, invite Him to remain in you with these verses.

God has chosen to make known among the Gentiles the glorious riches of this mystery: Christ in you, the hope of glory. (Colossians 1:27)

I have been crucified with Christ, and I no longer live, but Christ lives in me. The life I now live in the body, I live by faith in the Son of God, who loved me and gave himself for me. (Galatians 2:20)

I am the vine; you are the branches. If you remain in me and I in you, you will bear much fruit. (John 15:5)

Test yourselves. Do you not realize that Christ Jesus is in you? (2 Corinthians 13:5)

My children, with whom I travail again in birth until Christ is formed in you. (Galatians 4:19)

Now to him who is able to do immeasurably more than all we ask or imagine, according to his power that is at work within us. (Ephesians 3:20)

 Notes for reflection

Red Blood and White Robes

How does Christ's red blood make us white as snow? One would think that red blood would make us red, not white like snow. As always, the Bible is correct. Here is the medical explanation regarding how Christ's red blood can make us white.

There are two main types of blood cells: "red blood cells" and "white blood cells." The white blood cells are called "leukocytes." "Leuk" means white, and the cells are a white color. The job of each white blood cell is to destroy "sick" particles in our bodies. On the other hand, red blood cells give us life by supplying oxygen to our bodies.

The leukocytes' purpose is to kill bacteria, viruses, and cancer cells by miraculously sliding through blood vessel walls seeking harmful and dangerous items to be destroyed. Often white blood cells fight to their death as they kill bacteria, just as Jesus died to forgive our sins.

The analogy between Christ's blood and white blood cells is perfect! Christ's shed blood on the cross takes away our nasty sin while white blood cells take away our nasty bacteria. When we wash in Christ's blood, we become white as snow, just as our white blood cells make us white and clean from disease.

Come now, let us settle the matter, says the Lord. Though our sins are like scarlet, they shall be as white as snow, though they are red as crimson, they shall be like wool. (Isaiah 1:18)

They have washed their robes and made them white in the blood of the Lamb. (Revelation 7:14)

The blood of Jesus, his Son, purifies us from all sin. (1 John 1:7)

To Jesus Christ, who loves us and has freed us from our sins by his blood. (Revelation 1:5)

It is the blood that makes atonement for one's life. (Leviticus 17:11)

 **Notes for reflection**

Cones, Rods and the Holy Spirit

We cannot see the Holy Spirit, but if we look just a bit to the side, we often can see what He has been doing. We know that He is there. We can't see Him face to face, but we know that the Holy Spirit did the moving when He moves something.

Our eyes are a bit the same way. The "cones" in our eyes distinguish color and see directly where we are focusing. Unfortunately, the cones don't see well in dim light. On the other hand, the "rods" in our retina help us see black and white in the dim light just to the sides of where our eyes are focusing.

If you can't see a dim star in the night sky, focus a little to the side, and your peripheral vision with rods will see it. Similarly, if you can't read your watch in the dark, look a little to the side, and you may be able to see the watch hands better. If you can't see your way on a dark path, look a little bit to the side, and you'll see better what you couldn't see while focusing straight at it.

Similarly, keep watching for the Holy Spirit "God-sightings" in your life. You might see His powerful answers just to the side of your prayer. Sometimes the Holy Spirit moves in unexpected ways, far better than what you focused on in your prayer. It is exciting to keep your eyes open for Holy Spirit movements just to the side of your prayer requests!

But you will receive power when the Holy Spirit comes on you. (Acts 1:8)

The Spirit is given for the common good. To one, there is given through the Spirit wisdom, to another faith, to another gift of healing, miraculous powers, prophecy, and tongues. All these are the work of one and the same Spirit, and he distributes them to each one just as He determines. (1 Corinthians 12:7-11)

But the fruit of the Spirit is love, joy, peace, patience, kindness, goodness, faithfulness, gentleness, self-control. (Galatians 5:22,23)

For the Holy Spirit will teach you at that time what you should say. (Luke 12:12)

Likewise, the Spirit helps us in our weakness. For we do not know what to pray for as we ought, but the Spirit himself intercedes for us with groanings too deep for words. (Romans 8:26)

 Notes for reflection

What if you Sin after Confession?

Imagine that you confessed your sins this morning; however, you goof up and sin again in the afternoon. Your next scheduled time to ask for forgiveness is tomorrow morning during your devotions. What happens if you accidentally die before you ask for forgiveness for that most recent sin?

That one sin is still there and possibly not forgiven. Is that significant? No! Praise the Lord; He knows your heart.

Believe in the Lord Jesus, and you will be saved–you and your household. (Acts 16:32)

If you declare with your mouth, "Jesus is Lord" and believe in your heart that God raised him from the dead, you will be saved. (Romans 10:9)

If we confess our sins, he is faithful and just and will forgive us our sins and purify us from all unrighteousness. (1 John 1:9)

Whoever believes and is baptized will be saved. (Mark 16:16)

Be Perfect for a Moment!

Matthew 5:48 tells us to "Be perfect; therefore, as your heavenly Father is perfect." That is a challenging command. It is impossible to be perfect for a lifetime; we've all messed up. It's probably impossible to be perfect for a day and probably as well for an hour.

But

It might be possible to be perfect for one moment. Try this: ask for forgiveness of all sins, then ask Jesus to be Lord of your life. Tell the Lord you are 100% surrendered to Him and determine to do all that He asks you to do. With that being your heart's desire, hang in there for as many seconds as possible.

Praise the Lord! You were perfect for at least a few seconds by God's Grace. Congratulations, you did it! Doesn't that feel terrific to be perfect in the Lord? Now, if you could be perfect once a day, try to be perfect twice a day. Then, try to be perfect with God three times a day. How many times a day can you be perfect?

Be perfect; therefore, as your heavenly Father is perfect. (Matthew 5:48)

I urge you, brothers and sisters, in view of God's mercy, to offer your bodies as a living sacrifice, holy and pleasing to God—this is your true and proper worship. Do not conform to the pattern of this world, but be transformed by the renewing of your mind. Then you will be able to test and approve what God's will is—his good, pleasing, and perfect will. (Romans 12:1,2)

As he who called you is holy, you also be holy in all your conduct, since it is written, "You shall be holy, for I am holy." (Peter 1:15,16)

If we confess our sins, he is faithful and just and will forgive us our sins and purify us from all unrighteousness. (1 John 1:9)

Praise for God's Wealth

In the book of Revelation, we will be worshipping God because of His wealth. Just for a moment, try to imagine being in heaven as the Lord reveals His immense wealth to us. What could He show us that would result in great praise? What we experience in heaven will be far better than the following imaginary scenario.

Imagine being in heaven, where we are taken to see the "Gold Planet." This planet is about the earth's size, but instead of water and soil, it is composed entirely of sparkling, shiny polished 24 karat gold. The mountains, tall skyscrapers, playground equipment; everything is made out of pure gold; it's fantastic! It makes us wonder why we struggled so hard to get gold rings, gold necklaces, and all.

After a full day delighting in God's wealth, we are guided into a celestial theater that is "out of this world." There we see the Lord creating the gold planet. To our amazement, God reveals that the Gold Planet is small compared to the entire galaxy of billions of stars, countless worlds, and other constellations composed of pure 24 karat gold!

Then we all go back to our regular mansion in heaven, exclaiming about God's wealth!

In a loud voice they were saying: Worthy is the Lamb, who was slain, to receive power and wealth and wisdom and strength and honor and glory and praise! (Revelation 5:12)

He showed me the Holy City, Jerusalem, coming down out of heaven from God. It shone with the glory of God, and its brilliance was like that of a very precious jewel, like a jasper, clear as crystal. The wall was made of jasper, and the city of pure gold, as pure as glass. The foundations of the city walls were decorated with every kind of precious stone. (Revelation 21:10,18,19)

I pray that out of his glorious riches, he may strengthen you with power through his Spirit in your inner being so that Christ may dwell in your hearts through faith. (Ephesians 3:16,17)

I tell you, use worldly wealth to gain friends for yourselves, so that when it is gone, you will be welcomed into eternal dwellings. (Luke 16:9)

These have come so that the proven genuineness of your faith—of greater worth than gold—may result in praise, glory, and honor when Jesus Christ is revealed. (1 Peter 1:7)

Author's note: On the gold planet, dirt is very expensive and treasured because it grows flowers and vegetables!

Notes for reflection

Honor God

We will be thrilled to honor God in heaven! Honoring God is to recognize Him for what He has done. To honor God means to give Him respect, reverence, admiration, awe, praise, and obedience. "Honor" will be one of seven themes of adoration that will amaze us around His throne: "Praise, Honor, Glory, Majesty, Wisdom, Wealth and Power." We are to honor God with both our lips and our hearts.

It would be good to honor God now; a starting place would be for our salvation. Before the Lord saved us, He nudged our thoughts toward Him. Next, we experienced the Holy Spirit prompting us to ask for forgiveness for our sins. Finally, we said: "yes" for Jesus to be Lord of our life.

Once in heaven, It will become clear that the Lord gently brought circumstances and people into our lives. It may seem that we made a choice to become a Christian, but once in Heaven, it will be apparent that the Lord loved each of us, chose us, and gave us the courage to accept Christ as our Savior. That day was huge!

For eternity we each will honor God and praise Him for that and so much more. Jesus feels our love when we honor Him for what He has done. How are you doing honoring the Lord for what He has done in your life?

Praise be to the God and Father of our Lord Jesus Christ, who has blessed us in the heavenly realms with every spiritual blessing in Christ. For he chose us in him before the creation of the world to be holy and blameless in his sight. In love, he predestined us for adoption to sonship through Jesus Christ, in accordance with his pleasure and will. (Ephesians 1:3-5)

For it is by grace, you have been saved, through faith—and this is not from yourselves, it is the gift of God—not by works, so that no one can boast. (Ephesians 2:8,9)

Now to the King eternal, immortal, invisible, the only God, be honor and glory forever and ever. Amen. (1 Timothy 1:17)

You are worthy, our Lord and God, to receive glory and honor and power, for you created all things, and by your will, they were created and have their being. (Revelation 4:11)

Then I heard every creature in heaven saying: "To him who sits on the throne and to the Lamb be praise and honor and glory and power, forever and ever!" (Revelation 5:13)

 Notes for reflection

The Wisdom of God

God is all-wise and all-knowing; we know that. Nevertheless, some-times we wonder if His decisions are the best. When we get to Heav-en, our wondering will seem unfounded and foolish. But for now, we live in a fallen world with pain and suffering; Jesus died on the Cross, and bad things happen to good people. Some might question the wisdom of what is happening with all this pain and suffering. Do you sometimes?

For now, take great comfort in God's wisdom; He does everything in the wisest possible way! Forget all your questions about why so much pain. Instead, take great joy in God, who has done everything in the wisest way possible. The Lord loves each of us immensely, and we will have great joy as God reveals how our sufferings were God's most incredible plan for us.

Rejoice! God is Sovereign; He is in control. Everything is moving along just according to His plan. Our pain and sufferings are definite-ly in God's wise and loving control. "God is over all, through all, and in all." (Ephesians 4:6)

When we get to Heaven, we will be thrilled to explore God's wis-dom in our lives. For now, our challenge is to trust God, grow in faith, and keep on following Him.

Praise, Honor, and Glory; Majesty, Wisdom, and Power be to our God forever and ever. Amen! (Revelation 7:12)

For my thoughts are not your thoughts; neither are your ways my ways, declares the Lord. As the heavens are higher than the earth, so are my ways higher than your ways and my thoughts than your thoughts. (Isaiah 55:8,9)

Oh, the depth of the riches of the wisdom and knowledge of God! How unsearchable his judgments, and his paths beyond tracing out! (Romans 11:33)

For the foolishness of God is wiser than human wisdom. (1 Corinthians 1:25)

I form the light and create darkness, I bring prosperity and create disaster; I, the Lord, do all these things. (Isaiah 45:7)

But the wisdom that comes from heaven is first of all pure; then peace-loving, considerate, submissive, full of mercy and good fruit, impartial and sincere. (James 3:17)

And we know that in all things, God works for the good of those who love him, who have been called according to his purpose. (Romans 8:28)

 Notes for reflection

What Is God's Glory?

We talk about the "glory of God" but generally have difficulty explaining just what is God's "glory." The problem is that God's glory is beyond our comprehension. Nevertheless, let's try imagining it. Here is a starting point attempting to define God's "glory."

God's glory is infinite; it is limitless and endless. Therefore, there is no end to its increasing forever. Already that concept is beyond our comprehension, but it's a great start. Now try to imagine an epicenter from where God's glory radiates outward. At this point, it is easiest to imagine the sun radiating out the light depicted by the cover of this book. "God is light," so that is an excellent way to start picturing God's glory even if our sun is minimal compared to God.

Now light is just a small part of God's glory, so move on to "love." Visualize "love" radiating powerfully from that epicenter. That "love" is so powerful and wonderful that it would take an eternity to understand it. Consider this exercise during your next prayer time: imagine waves of God's supernatural love flowing out from that epicenter towards you.

Next, replace "light" and "love" with God's infinite "beauty" emanating from His throne. At this point, we are overwhelmed with God's glory, but there is so much more to behold. There remains: "holiness, "wisdom," "majesty," "wealth," and "power" all interwoven into God's glory. They are beaming out beyond our finite mind's ability to comprehend.

In your devotions, pray for just one of these qualities shining toward you powerfully; ever-increasing "light," "love," "beauty," "wisdom," "holiness," "majesty," "wealth," and "power"! For eternity, we will be thrilled to experience God's magnificent "glory"!

Then Jesus said, "Did I not tell you that if you believe, you will see the glory of God?" (John 11:40)

Then I heard every creature in heaven and on earth saying: "To him who sits on the throne and to the Lamb be praise, honor, glory, power, wealth, wisdom and strength forever and ever!" (Revelation 5:12,13)

The Holy City shone with the glory of God, and its brilliance was like that of a very precious jewel, like a jasper, clear as crystal. The city does not need the sun or the moon to shine on it, for the glory of God gives it light (Revelation 21:11, 23)

The heavens declare the glory of God; the skies proclaim the work of his hands. Day after day, they pour forth speech; night after night, they reveal knowledge, their voice goes out into all the earth. (Psalm 19:1-4)

And my God will meet all your needs according to the riches of his glory in Christ Jesus. (Philippians 4:19)

Rejoice in the hope of the glory of God. (Romans 5:2)

 **Notes for reflection**

A Little can Make a Huge Difference

Sometimes the smallest effort can make all the difference in our lives. Stay fifteen minutes extra at your new job without pay; you may get promoted above all the rest. Write a thank-you note to someone who has helped you; you may "make their day." Take an extra ten minutes to review your exam; you may be able to correct some errors. Each small act may be that which makes the difference!

The thief on the Cross showed a spark of compassion toward Jesus. He did so little extra, but it made such a huge difference that he went to be with Jesus in heaven for eternity!

We will never know how Jesus will use just a small effort. Little things and acts of kindness will go a long way toward serving Him and serving others. The Holy Spirit can make a little spark of love grow into a FOREST FIRE. We can let our love shine out to Jesus and others by doing little things that make a big difference.

Then the thief said, "Jesus, remember me when you come into your kingdom." Jesus answered him, "Truly, I tell you, today you will be with me in paradise." (Luke 23:42,43)

"Those who were hired last worked only one hour, and you have paid them equal to us who have borne the burden of the work and the heat of the day." But he answered one of them; "I am not unfair to you, friend. Didn't you agree to work for a denarius? Take your pay and go. I want to give the one who was hired last the same as I gave you." (Matthew 20:10-15)

Believe in the Lord Jesus, and you will be saved—you and your household. (Acts 16:31)

Get into Heaven!

Get yourself saved; that's such a "no brainer." Heaven is free; it is terrific. Don't let anything rob you of unimaginable love and joy. Heaven is incredible compared to going to hell. No matter what the cost, GO TO HEAVEN!

The Christian life, without question, is a better life than the non-Christian alternative. Talk with Christians about their experience before and after. Consider also the disasters non-Christians get caught in, that by God's grace didn't happen to you! To be a follower of Jesus is not always easy, but it is far better. There are so many benefits to getting saved early in life and then seeing what adventure God can cook up for you. The sooner you become a Christian, the sooner you reap this "more abundant life" and receive God's power in your life.

It is difficult to understand why people procrastinate becoming followers of Jesus. It's risky; no one knows when they will die. So many lovely people keep putting off getting saved until tomorrow or next month or until they retire. What's wrong with people? Why are so many waiting?

In heaven, there will be:

1. Inexpressible and glorious joy to the max. (1 Peter 1:8)
2. Love, joy, peace (Galatians 5:22)
3. The side that is winning. "God Almighty" is quoted 125 times in the Bible
4. Serious pleasures forever throughout eternity. (Psalm 16:11)
5. No more tears, death, or pain (Revelation 21:4)

They know nothing, they understand nothing; their eyes are plastered over so they cannot see, and their minds closed so they cannot understand. See, darkness covers the earth, and thick darkness is over the peoples. (Isaiah 44:18) (Isaiah 60:2)

If the blind lead the blind, both will fall into a pit. (Matthew 15:14)

I tell you, now is the time of God's favor, now is the day of salvation. (2 Corinthians 6:2)

If you declare with your mouth, "Jesus is Lord," and believe in your heart that God raised him from the dead, you will be saved. (Romans 10:9,10)

Believe in the Lord Jesus, and you will be saved—you and your household. (Acts 16:31)

You love him and are filled with an inexpressible and glorious joy, for you are receiving the end result of your faith, the salvation of your souls. (1 Peter 1:8,9)

He will wipe every tear from their eyes. There will be no more death or mourning or crying or pain. (Revelation 21:4)

 Notes for reflection

Pack a Punch with "I Love You, Jesus!"

There are many different levels of intensity to pray, "I Love You, Jesus." One way is without excitement because it's routine, and you say it often. The opposite method is to exclaim, "I Love You, Jesus" with profound emotion! The same message occurs, one relatively flat and the other with great feeling. Is there any difference between these two messages when they arrive at Jesus in heaven?

We all know that It might be a stretch to love the Lord with high emotion all the time; that's okay. Just love with whatever feeling you can generate. Don't get too bent out of shape about your lack of emotional intensity. Remember, it's much better to love God with lukewarm emotion than not to love Him at all.

However, there might be some helpful methods to generate more love if you wish to do so. One suggestion might be to find something that brought you to tears in the past. The "Footprints in the Sand" poem works for some. Perhaps listen to your favorite Christian song that emotionally touches you. Listen to it often and embrace loving the Lord during the song.

Here is a challenge: think about what you love more than anything else in life; your family or car or spouse or ????? Now love the Lord just a bit more than the object you love so dearly. You can do it! If not able, ask the Lord for help. Do you have any other suggestions on generating more "Love for the Lord" in your prayer time and your life?

Emote what you can. Jesus will understand; don't give up!

Jesus replied: "Love the Lord your God with all your heart and with all your soul and with all your mind." (Matthew 22:37)

During the days of Jesus' life on earth, he offered up prayers and petitions with fervent cries and tears to the one who could save him from death, and he was heard because of his reverent submission. (Hebrews 5:7)

The fervent prayer of a righteous person is powerful and effective. (James 5:16)

Likewise, the Spirit also helps in our weaknesses. For we do not know what we should pray for as we ought, but the Spirit Himself makes intercession for us with groanings which cannot be uttered. (Romans 8:26)

 Notes for reflection

How can I Increase my Prayer Power?

I often pray too routinely and just pray for easy things. How can I increase my prayer power? "The earnest prayer of a righteous person has great power and produces incredible results." (James 5:16 NLT)

God can unleash tremendous power in answering even the weakest prayer. On the other hand, there are biblical suggestions to increase the power of prayer. What do you think of these ideas?

1. Get to know God well. He is the one who will be answering your prayers.
2. Receive personal forgiveness.
3. Pray continually. The more times you pray, the more power is released.
4. Have others join in prayer; where two or more are gathered, the Lord is there.
5. Increased fervency might help – tears and intensity.
6. Use the Bible's promises with your prayers.
7. Lay hands on the person for whom you are praying.
8. Anoint with oil and try fasting.
9. Go to the elders of your church and ask them to pray.
10. Pray for more faith and believe that you have received it.

Or perhaps, just forget the above long list and pray to the Creator of the Universe with all your heart. He will listen, and His answers are incredible!

Take delight in the Lord, and he will give you the desires of your heart. (Psalm 37:4)

I keep asking that God may give you the Spirit of wisdom and revelation so that you may know him better. I pray that you might know his incomparably great power for us who believe. (Ephesians 1:17-19)

Pray continually, give thanks in all circumstances; for this is God's will for you in Christ Jesus. (1 Thessalonians 5:17,18)

Again, truly I tell you that if two of you on earth agree about anything they ask for, it will be done for them by my Father in heaven. For where two or three gather in my name, there am I with them. (Matthew 18:19,20)

During the days of Jesus' life on earth, he offered up prayers and petitions with fervent cries and tears to the one who could save him from death, and he was heard because of his reverent submission. (Hebrews 5:7)

Let them call the elders of the church to pray over them and anoint them with oil in the name of the Lord. The prayer of a righteous person is powerful and effective. (James 5:14-16)

Therefore, I tell you, whatever you ask for in prayer, believe that you have received it, and it will be yours. (Mark 11:24, Matthew 21:22)

 Notes for reflection

Oops – A Big Mistake

What if you make a big mistake in church? You mistakenly put a $50 bill in the offering plate but meant it to be a five-dollar bill? Does the Lord give you credit for the $50, or do you only get credit for five dollars because that's what you meant to put in?

Here are two possible considerations:

1. Pray that the Lord will give you $50 credit even if you initially meant it to be only $5. Ask the Lord to accept your $50 as a cheerful donation. That would solve the problem, and I think the Lord would switch it in His books.

2. Pray that the Lord will use your $50 in amazing ways for His glory. Throw Ephesians 3:20 into this financial equation; "Now to him who is able to do immeasurably more than you ask or imagine according to his power that is in you." Maybe that implies that even if you only get credit for the five dollars, it will be expanded "immeasurably beyond what you can imagine."

When it's all said and done, next time, throw in another $50 bill. Who knows; it may expand possibly to $5 billion over the next 10,000 years in heaven, and even more later.

Each of you should give what you have decided in your heart to give, not reluctantly or under compulsion, for God loves a cheerful giver. (2 Corinthians 9:7)

Sell your possessions and give to the poor. Provide purses for yourselves that will not wear out, a treasure in heaven that will never fail, where no thief comes near and no moth destroys. (Luke 12:33)

But a poor widow came and put in two very small copper coins, worth only a few cents. Jesus said, "Truly I tell you, this poor widow has put more into the treasury than all the others. They all gave out of their wealth, but she put in everything—all she had to live on out of her poverty." (Mark 12:42-44)

Bring the whole tithe into the storehouse, that there may be food in my house. "Test me in this," says the Lord Almighty, "and see if I will not throw open the floodgates of heaven and pour out so much blessing that there will not be room enough to store it." (Malachi 3:10)

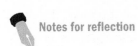 Notes for reflection

The Spiritual Fly Swatter

What do you do if a distracting thought comes into your mind when you are praying? I suggest that you get a "spiritual fly swatter" and swat that distraction.

Daydreaming about work or other anxieties frequently disrupts our prayer times. With a little touch of anger, grab that swatter, and smack that distraction. Then calmly choose to go back to prayer. The more gossipy the thought is, the harder you should swat. It's also okay to say "sorry, Lord"; after all, you would apologize if you were distracted while talking to your human friend.

Many prayer warriors notice that they have more distracting thoughts in the evening because the day's distractions and list of "things to do" are swirling around in their minds. What time of day works best for you to pray?

The location where you pray also makes a difference. A small quiet room seems about right, but a busy beach with much activity doesn't work as well. Lights out may work best for some, but be cautious about falling asleep. Sleep is also a distraction, but the fly swatter often can't be found in time, it seems.

If the distraction is from the Lord wanting you to pray for something else, hold back on the fly swatter. Some people like a verse on their fly swatter. What words would you put on yours? Here are two Bible verses that might work well:

#1 The prayer of a righteous person is powerful and effective. (James 5:16)

#2 Ask, and it will be given to you. (Matthew 7:7)

Practice with your spiritual fly swatter; you might find it very helpful. Use it often!

But when you pray, go into your room, close the door and pray to your Father, who is unseen. Then your Father, who sees what is done in secret, will reward you. And when you pray, do not keep on babbling like pagans, for they think they will be heard because of their many words. Do not be like them, for your Father knows what you need before you ask him. (Matthew 6:6-8)

Likewise, the Spirit also helps in our weaknesses. For we do not know what we should pray for as we ought, but the Spirit Himself makes intercession for us with groanings which cannot be uttered. (Romans 8: 26–27)

 Notes for reflection

Spiritual Protection

Did you know that it is wartime on planet earth? "Be alert and of sober mind. Your enemy, the devil prowls around like a roaring lion looking for someone to devour." (1 Peter 5:8) The Bible tells us to put on the armor of God and be strong in the Lord and in His mighty power. Here are some practical suggestions for protecting yourself from evil.

Claim every area that you enter to be under the Lordship of Jesus Christ. Claim the doctor's office, your workplace, the bus, the classroom, your home, the birthday party, etc. Ask the Lord to be in control of each place you enter.

Here are four different "warfare prayers" that you might pray to protect yourself:

#1 Cleanse sin from the area.

#2 Make Satan flee from the site and put Jesus in control.

#3 Put a spiritual "hedge of protection" there, so it is safe for you.

#4 Put on the Armor of God.

#1 Cover yourself, others, and items with the blood of Jesus Christ. If you cover yourself with Christ's blood, God no longer sees sin; instead, God sees His Son.

But if we walk in the light, the blood of Jesus, his Son, purifies us from all sin. (1 John 1:7)

We have the confidence to enter the Most Holy Place by the blood of Jesus. (Hebrews 10:19)

They triumphed over Satan by the blood of the Lamb. (Revelation 12:11)

Jesus came to reconcile all things through his blood shed on the cross. (Colossians 1:20)

#2 Resist Satan so that He will flee from you, others, and the area in which you are concerned. When finished resisting Satan, ask Jesus Christ to be the supreme authority there.

Submit yourselves, then, to God. Resist the devil, and he will flee from you. Draw near to God, and He will draw near to you. (James 4:7)

The reason the Son of God appeared was to destroy the devil's work. (1 John 3:8)

Jesus, who is in you, is greater than the one who is in the world. (1 John 4:4)

Lead us not into temptation but deliver us from the evil one. (Matthew 6:13)

#3 Pray that God will put a "hedge of protection" surrounding you. Have you not put a hedge of protection around him and his household and everything he has? (Job 1:10)

#4 Finally, **be strong** in the Lord and in his mighty power. Put on the full armor of God. Stand firm then with the belt of truth, the breastplate of righteousness, feet fitted with the gospel of peace, the shield of faith, the helmet of salvation, and the sword of the Spirit, which is the word of God. (Ephesians 6:10-17)

 Notes for reflection

It is all about your "Love Score"

Some folks did so well in school and always got good grades. If you are one of those types, you might like to grade your activities each day and get excellent marks!

Life is about "love," so we will try to determine your "love score." Jesus came to make "life abundant" (John 10:10b), so life should include lots of love! Apostle Paul encourages us to "live a life of loving one another," and "let all you do, be done in love." In summary, God is love, and we are to be lovers like Him. So here is the fun exercise:

Think about yesterday and give yourself a grade for how you "loved God" and "loved others": 10 for great love; 0 for no love. Any love counts, and any love expressed to the Lord should be given double points.

Here is an example tally for my "love score" yesterday:
- Had devotions = 10 points
- Prayed before each meal X 3 = 3 points
- Saw beautiful sunset and thanked God for it = 5 points
- Smiled and encouraged cashier at grocery store = 1 point
- Prayed for victims' families after the bad news on TV = 3 points
- Chose to do something better than watching a questionable TV show = 4 points
- Had a "pity party" while thinking negative thoughts = Minus 5

So there you have it. I accumulated a "love score" yesterday of 26 and a minus 5, which gave me a love score of 21 for yesterday. Any score above 5 is passing; any score above 10 is an A. Any score above 20 is A+ Tally up your love score for yesterday. How did you do?

Jesus replied, "Love the Lord your God with all your heart and with all your soul and with all your mind. And the second is like it: Love your neighbor as yourself." (Matthew 22:37-39)

Do everything in love. Love your neighbor as yourself. (1 Corinthians 16:14, James 2:8)

God is love. Whoever lives in love lives in God, and God in them. (1 John 4:16)

Dear friends, let us love one another, for love comes from God. Everyone who loves has been born of God and knows God. Whoever does not love does not know God because God is love. (1 John 4:7,8)

If your love score is like mine some days and not so good, take heart and read about God's great mercy:
The Lord is full of compassion and mercy. (James 5:11)

 Notes for reflection

Have You Turned Vertical?

Have you turned vertical? As people get older, they generally change their focus from horizontal thinking to more vertical thinking. Let me explain: When in high school and college, most attention is horizontal, aimed at relationships with peers, grades, and getting a job. Then, there's often marriage, kids, financial survival to focus on; it's all pretty horizontal.

But looking up to God is quite a vertical gaze. It's indeed beautiful when some young people start looking up to God at an early age. Even so, there are many horizontal distractions with which most young folks deal.

As one gets older, however, more of the horizontal life becomes history. The job gets more routine, and there's more time to look upward toward God. When friends pass away, or severe disease threatens, people increase their vertical gaze remarkably!

Here is good advice: As early in life as possible, maximize your vertical gaze to the Lord. You will reap the more abundant life and His great benefits sooner. Strengthen your vertical gaze; it's not only the correct thing to do but has superb rewards now and forever!

The prayer of a righteous person is powerful and effective. (James 5:16)

Command those who are rich in this present world not to be arrogant or put their hope in wealth, which is so uncertain, but to put their hope in God, who richly provides us with everything for our enjoyment. Command them to do good, to be rich in good deeds, and to be generous and willing to share. In this way, they will lay up treasure for themselves as a firm foundation for the coming age so that they may take hold of the life that is truly life. (1 Timothy 6:17-19)

I have come that they may have life and have it to the full. (John 10:10b)

Whoever wants to be my disciple must deny themselves and take up their cross daily and follow me. (Luke 9:23)

 Notes for reflection

Aim for Pleasure

One goal in life is to aim for your greatest pleasure. I know that sounds wrong. Nevertheless, we all strive for greater joy and happiness. Sometimes it takes earnest hard work to get there.

If you desire to have the most joy possible in life, here is a great suggestion: Follow Jesus to find this joy and happiness. Line up on God's side quickly and ask Jesus to be your boss. He will guide you to make the best decisions and give you added strength when you need it. He will thrill you with answers to your prayer. All these benefits will result in the most exciting and joyful life possible.

Realize that some of your happiness includes godly escapes from sinful pits that many fall into without Jesus. Some pits are really "the pits" and can destroy your joy. Switch from "your way" to "God's way." Jesus promises a more abundant life and will help you maximize love, joy, peace, kindness, and goodness.

When difficulties come, realize they are part of God's mysterious plan. Life with Christ is the very best deal on planet earth. The greatest pleasure during this life is found in Jesus. Don't forget that when death comes, you are destined for pleasures at God's right hand for eternity.

I, Jesus, have come that they may have life and have it to the full. (John 10:10b)

But the fruit of the Spirit is love, joy, peace, patience, kindness, goodness, faithfulness, gentleness, and self-control. (Galatians 5:22,23)

You believe in Jesus and are filled with an inexpressible and glorious joy, for you are receiving the end result of your faith, the salvation of your souls. (1 Peter 1:8,9)

You make known to me the path of life; you will fill me with joy in your presence, with eternal pleasures at your right hand. (Psalm 16:11)

 Notes for reflection

Testing or Tempting?

Are you being tempted or tested? There is a vast difference. Satan tempts us, but the Lord tests us. Both may feel somewhat similar, however.

Here are some clues to tell the difference. Satan's temptations generally entice a person to sin. His temptations often have a delicious immediate payoff, but they frequently demand some compromise to one's character. Beware of making "deals" that don't seem quite right. The benefit that Satan promises usually fails; it was just a deception from the beginning.

We all know that God doesn't tempt us, but He does test us. God tests us to prove that we love Him and will trust Him through the test. We can prove to Him and Satan that we are faithful. Testing is God trusting us to make the right choice.

No testing seems pleasant, but to pass the test and get an "A" is exciting! When you see the Lord's testing coming to you, pray hard, and give the Lord your best effort. Each of the Lord's tests for us is measured, controlled, and fits us perfectly. Ask the Lord for strength if you feel the intensity of testing is too much. With God's power and grace, you can do it. Aim for an "A plus"!

When tempted, no one should say, "God is tempting me." For God cannot be tempted by evil, nor does he tempt anyone; but each person is tempted when they are dragged away by their own evil desire and enticed. Then, after desire has conceived, it gives birth to sin; and sin, when it is full-grown, gives birth to death. (James 1:13-15)

The Lord, your God, is testing you to find out whether you love him with all your heart and with all your soul. (Deuteronomy 13:3)

Because he himself suffered when he was tempted, he is able to help those who are being tempted. (Hebrews 2:18)

Consider it pure joy, my brothers and sisters, whenever you face trials of many kinds because you know that the testing of your faith produces perseverance. Let perseverance finish its work so that you may be mature and complete, not lacking anything. (James 1:2-4)

Dear friends, do not be surprised at the fiery ordeal that has come on you to test you, as though something strange were happening to you. But rejoice inasmuch as you participate in the sufferings of Christ, so that you may be overjoyed when his glory is revealed. (1 Peter 4:12,13)

Resist Satan, and he will flee from you. (James 4:7)

No temptation has overtaken you, except what is common to mankind. God is faithful; he will not let you be tempted beyond what you can bear. But when you are tempted, he will also provide a way out so that you can endure it. (1 Corinthians 10:13)

Blessed is the one who endures trials because when he has stood the test, he will receive the crown of life that God has promised to those who love him. (James 1:12)

 **Notes for reflection**

Dogs with Collars do Best

Dogs with collars do the best. I don't know if my dog likes her collar. She doesn't seem to mind when I put it on her, and she wears it without complaining. The dog tags ring and make music when she runs, letting us know she is near and will protect us. I think she likes the collar!

The collar has also saved her life many times when running into the road or running toward other dogs. Some dogs look friendly but might chop her head off if she got too close. Her collar keeps her out of lots of trouble, especially when away from home.

The Ten Commandments are somewhat like a collar that we followers of Jesus wear. Some folks say there are 10,000 laws in our government to enforce the Ten Commandments. What do you think about the Ten Commandments being an excellent "collar"? Let me take "collar" out of the above paragraphs and switch in "The Ten Commandments" and apply it to us! Here it is:

"I don't know if I like the Ten Commandments. But I don't seem to mind when I follow them and wouldn't complain about them. The "Big Ten" lets others know that I'm safe and don't want to steal, kill, or take their married partners away. The Ten Commandments are beautiful music to many people, and they trust me. I think I actually like the Ten Commandments!"

"The 'Big Ten' has saved my life many times, running into the road or befriending people who look friendly but might chop off my head if I got too close. The Ten Commandments keep me out of trouble, especially when away from home."

If your "Ten Commandment collar" is too heavy, try this smaller "royal purple collar" on for size. This purple collar is pretty much the same, just a lot lighter: "Love God and love your neighbor." If you would prefer something very small, this tiny "pink collar" works okay, but it's not as strong and won't help you if you are in a big dogfight: "Do to others as you would have them do to you."

Enjoy and take pride in wearing "The Big Ten" collar!

The Ten Commandments:

1. You shall have no other gods before me.

2. You shall not make idols.

3. You shall not misuse the name of the Lord your God.

4. Remember the Sabbath day by keeping it holy.

5. Honor your father and your mother.

6. You shall not murder.

7. You shall not commit adultery.

8. You shall not steal.

9. You shall not give false testimony against your neighbor.

10. You shall not covet your neighbor's house, wife, donkey (car), or anything that belongs to your neighbor.

Notes for reflection

When did Jesus Realize He was God?

Three years of age is the earliest people can remember being alive unless they see a picture of themselves to imagine remembering earlier. How old was Jesus when He realized that He was God? At five years of age, many children make a confession of faith, accepting Jesus as Lord and Savior. Mary and Joseph must have told Jesus at a very early age about His extraordinary birth with angels, shepherds, and their escape to Egypt.

When Jesus was 12 years old, Mary and Joseph mistakenly left Him in Jerusalem and three days later found Him talking with the teachers. At that time, many people believe that He must have known who He was and that He was mentioned in many of the Old Testament prophecies.

Jesus never sinned. Did He ever steal a cookie or beat up his brothers in a mean way? "No!" Did Jesus always get perfect scores in elementary school? "No." Did He ever mistakenly cut a board too short while helping His carpenter father? "Yes."

Here's my take on it; what do you think? The Holy Spirit was powerful with Jesus and gave Him a spiritually wonderful childhood protecting Him from sinning. We don't know whether He was a colicky baby, but early on, the Holy Spirit gave Him a great love for God His Father and godly responses to life situations. His spiritual IQ was miraculous; He knew that He could perform miracles before performing his first public miracle, turning water into wine.

It is impressive that in heaven, nine months before His birth, Jesus set aside His mighty power and glory! He took off His omnipotence, omnipresence, and omniscience. Then He permitted the Holy Spirit to miraculously transfer Him into Mary's surrogate womb, to be delivered nine months later.

After His birth, He grew with the Holy Spirit's help, to understand who He was; Jesus Christ, the Son of God. As the Holy Spirit gave Him insight into Holy Scripture, Jesus grew in wisdom and stature. He talked closely with His Father knowing and preparing to die for the sins of each of us. JESUS MUST LOVE US SO MUCH MORE THAN WE REALIZE!

And the child grew and became strong; he was filled with wisdom, and the grace of God was on him. (Luke 2:40)

When he was twelve years old, Jesus' parents went up to the festival, according to the custom. After the festival was over, while his parents were returning home, the boy Jesus stayed behind in Jerusalem, but they were unaware of it. After three days, they found him in the temple courts, sitting among the teachers, listening to them and asking them questions. Everyone who heard him was amazed at his understanding and his answers. When his parents saw him, His mother said to him, "Son, Your father and I have been anxiously searching for you." "Why were you searching for me?" He asked. "Didn't you know I had to be in my Father's house?" (Luke 2:42-49)

Who, being in very nature God, did not consider equality with God something to be used to his own advantage; rather, he made himself nothing by taking the very nature of a servant, being made in human likeness. (Philippians 2:6,7)

For the joy set before him, he endured the cross, scorning its shame, and sat down at the right hand of the throne of God. (Hebrews 12:2)

Notes for reflection

What did Jesus Look Like?

What did Jesus look like? I would love to see the real Jesus. Galilean men were about 5 foot 5 inches tall. There is no mention in the Bible that He was unusually tall or handsome. Jesus probably wasn't obese nor skinny either. Isaiah mentions, "He had no beauty or majesty to attract us to him, nothing in his appearance that we should desire him." (Isaiah 53:2)

Jesus probably looked quite "regular" without unusual peculiarities such as a limp or stutter or dark blue eyes. Did he get perfect scores on all of his tests and win the city wrestling title every time? "No." He probably stubbed his toe on rocks and caught viral bronchitis, just like each of us.

When He left Heaven, He set aside His mighty power and glory and limited Himself to using only the Holy Spirit's power. We each are in the same situation as Jesus; we are regular in appearance and also need to rely totally upon the Holy Spirit's power. Like Jesus, we also have a destiny to fulfill prepared for us long before we were born.

We are limited by our earthly bodies and activities unless, of course, the Lord calls us to do something miraculous, just like Jesus did. But that is the point: by God's Grace, with the power of the Holy Spirit, we can pray for miracles. That is what Jesus did!

For we are God's handiwork, created in Christ Jesus to do good works, which God prepared in advance for us to do. (Ephesians 2:10)

Jesus made himself nothing by taking the very nature of a servant, being made in human likeness. And being found in appearance as a man, he humbled himself. (Philippians 2:7,8)

Very truly I tell you, whoever believes in me will do the works I have been doing, and they will do even greater things than these, because I am going to the Father. (John 14:12)

And I will do whatever you ask in my name, so that the Father may be glorified in the Son. You may ask me for anything in my name, and I will do it. (John 14:13,14)

Jesus looked at them and said, "With man, this is impossible, but with God all things are possible." (Matthew 19:26)

 Notes for reflection

Celebrate "Tetelestai" in your Life

Celebrate "tetelestai" in your life; it often means that something better is coming. Tetelestai is a Greek word that means "it is finished" and was the last word that Jesus said from the Cross. He suffered terrible agony, and with that word, He bowed His head and gave up His Spirit. Life got much better for Jesus after He finished. He was set free. Memorize "tetelestai" so that you can use it often when you finish a frightening, difficult time.

While nothing we experience is as painful as Jesus' death on the Cross, many things in our lives finally come to an end; praise the Lord for that! After a big, exhausting day, crawl into the sheets and whisper "tetelestai." When your scary interview or your annual review is over, say "tetelestai" and breathe a sigh of relief.

After "tetelestai - it is finished," it often means that something better is coming. For Jesus, it meant He was headed to Heaven soon. When you finish your challenging event, you are probably looking forward to something much better also.

Take great joy saying "tetelestai" now and then in your daily life; in fact, say it often. Remember that Jesus was the first to say it at His triumph on the cross. A new time was coming for HIm, and the same is true for you after finishing something challenging!

Jesus said, "It is finished." With that, he bowed his head and gave up his spirit. (John 19:30)

Tetelestai – Wikipedia – The title comes from the Greek word τετέλεσται (tetelestai) meaning "it is finished," which are the last words of Jesus on the cross.

A Really Grumpy Discouraging Day

What do you do on a really grumpy, "everything's going wrong" day? Here is the Bible challenge: "Rejoice in the Lord always. I will say it again: Rejoice!" (Philippians 4:4)

I tried and almost failed. Here are four things I tried:

1. "It could be so, so much worse!" That's true, but thinking that didn't help.
2. There is the consolation that tomorrow will be a new day, and things will possibly get better. That didn't work because I should be rejoicing right now, not waiting for tomorrow.
3. An ice cream sundae right now might help, or take a nap, a backrub?
4. Imagine a quick trip to hell, where there are darkness and pain, followed by a short trip to heaven where there are pleasures forever at Christ's right hand.

Wow!!!! That worked for me. Now I am rejoicing; again, I say: I am rejoicing!

If your hand causes you to stumble, cut it off. It is better for you to enter life maimed than with two hands to go into hell, where the fire never goes out. (Mark 9:43)

Father Abraham, have pity on me and send Lazarus to dip the tip of his finger in water and cool my tongue because I am in agony in this fire. (Luke 16: 24)

Do not be afraid of those who kill the body but cannot kill the soul. Instead, be afraid of the One who can destroy both soul and body in hell. (Matthew 10:28)

You make known to me the path of life; you will fill me with joy in your presence, with eternal pleasures at your right hand. (Psalm 16:11)

However, as it is written: What no eye has seen, what no ear has heard, and what no human mind has conceived—the things God has prepared for those who love him. (1 Corinthians 2:9)

 Notes for reflection

Be Brave, Be Courageous!

Be brave; be courageous even though it is scary. Risk is involved, and failure is always a possibility. It is always easier to do nothing or something comfortable with less risk.

On the other hand, if we will be brave and take some risks for the Lord, we will be amazed at what He will do! "No pain, no gain," some say. Jesus took significant risks for us and may call us to do the same for Him and others. Take heart! If He calls you, He will be with you!

Be strong and courageous. Do not be afraid; do not be discouraged, for the Lord your God will be with you wherever you go. (Joshua 1:9)

Ask anything in my name, and I will do it that the Lord may be glorified. (John 14:14)

Now to him who is able to do immeasurably more than all we ask or imagine, according to his power that is at work within us. (Ephesians 3:20)

For everyone who asks receives; the one who seeks finds; and to the one who knocks, the door will be opened. (Matthew 7:8)

Truly I tell you, if you have faith as small as a mustard seed, you can say to this mountain, "Move from here to there," and it will move. Nothing will be impossible for you. (Matthew 17:20)

You do not have because you do not ask God. (James 4:2)

I can do all things through Him who strengthens me. (Philippians 4:13)

For God gave us a spirit not of fear, but of power and love and self-control. (2 Timothy 1:7)

Finally, be strong in the Lord and in the strength of his might. (Ephesians 6:10)

For nothing will be impossible with God. (Luke 1:37)

What then shall we say to these things? If God is for us, who can be against us? (Romans 8:31)

And my God will supply every need of yours according to his riches in glory in Christ Jesus. (Philippians 4:19)

He who is in you is greater than he who is in the world. (1 John 4:4)

 **Notes for reflection**

Five Billion Years From Now!

Our sun blows up in five billion years eliminating earth. Let's look at our lives beyond those five billion years in the far distant future. Here is what I see us doing:

We all will be living luxuriously in heaven with the Father, Jesus, and the Holy Spirit. Life in the New Jerusalem has been our home base on planet earth. There is no concern about earth because we are with the Lord. He has provided another New Jerusalem, which is far more glorious, in a new location!

Our unique relationship being the bride of Christ has been exceptional and beyond description. Our love for Him has grown and grown and is "new every morning." The "robes of righteousness" we wear dramatically change depending on the circumstances we find ourselves in; heavenly beaches, concerts, or outer space regions. Even though we have experienced five billion years of incredible loving relationships and other thrills, we know that a future "eternity" awaits us with ever greater unfolding grandeur.

The old "earth life" seems like just yesterday, and our hearts are filled with gratitude as we see how the Lord brought us, by His Grace, into a loving relationship with Him. From Heaven's perspective, our earthly disasters and problems appear so different as we see the Lord's gentle touch nudging us closer and closer to Him.

Most of all, we are amazed at how the incredibly short "years of earth life" determined our eternity of glorious joy with the Lord and each other. It's fantastic. It's supernatural. It is inexpressible and magnificent beyond words.

As most of us look back and discuss our earth life together, there tends to be only one regret. We all feel it and tend not to "talk about it." As you know, we don't need to "talk" in heaven because our thoughts simply pass between each of us. The "one regret" is an inward wish that we would have done so much more back on earth; we could have used God's power tools of praying and loving so much more powerfully.

"Regret" always, by God's extraordinary grace, immediately turns into "thankfulness" and deep gratitude for what the Lord did accomplish in our past lives. There is so much more to describe. Looking back at the last five billion years of God's wisdom and love is great, but I can't wait for tomorrow's adventure!

However, as it is written: "What no eye has seen, what no ear has heard, and what no human mind has conceived"— the things God has prepared for those who love him. (1 Corinthians 2:9)

Though you have not seen him, you love him; and even though you do not see him now, you believe in him and are filled with an inexpressible and glorious joy. (1 Peter 1:8)

You will fill me with joy in your presence, with eternal pleasures at your right hand. (Psalm 16:11)

My Father's house has many rooms, and if I go to prepare a place for you, I will come back and take you to be with me that you also may be where I am. (John 14:2,3)

Notes for reflection

See the next page for a cerificate to make your commitment to the new life with Jesus that this book has called you to.

1. Admit: "I am a sinner."
2. Jesus, please forgive my sins.
3. I believe that Jesus Christ died for me on the Cross and rose from the grave.
4. I invite you, Jesus Christ, to be my Lord and Savior.

Pray:

Dear Lord Jesus,

I know that I am a sinner and need Your forgiveness.

I believe that You died for my sins. Forgive my sins.

I now invite You to come into my heart and life.

I want to trust and follow You as Lord and Savior.

In Jesus' Name.

Amen

Date _____

Name _____

Why This Book Is Written

The primary purpose of this book is so that you can help your friend get into heaven! Each chapter is to "help you help them" become a "Jesus follower." What's the plan? What can you possibly say to encourage someone to "love Jesus?"

After you have prayed for your friend, you might bring up one of the topics in this book. See what your friend says about it. Your enthusiasm might be "catchy." Then pray, pray, pray, and see what the Holy Spirit will do!

When it's all said and done, you've encouraged your friend to become a follower of Jesus. It is exciting, and he or she might begin an adventure of a lifetime. Why not spend eternity together? In time, perhaps your friend will know a friend who wants to go to heaven also!

You have read the following verses often in this book, so you might as well memorize them. You might need them today!

This means that anyone who belongs to Christ has become a new person. The old life is gone; a new life has begun! (2 Corinthians 5:17 NLT)

If you declare with your mouth, "Jesus is Lord," and believe in your heart that God raised him from the dead, you will be saved. (Romans 10: 9,10)

Believe in the Lord Jesus, and you will be saved—you and your household. (Acts 16:1)

Nail It Down Once and for All

After following Jesus for a few years, I desired to have a signed and dated document to remind me of my commitment. I wanted my own "official document" stating that once and for all, I have entirely asked Jesus to forgive my sins and be Lord of my life. I made a statement, signed it, and am so glad I did. The following is a document you might use to verify that you have received Jesus as your Savior and Lord once and for all.

Here is the "small print" relating that you are becoming a follower of Jesus:

If we confess our sins, he is faithful and just and will forgive us our sins and purify us from all unrighteousness. (1 John 1:9)

If you declare with your mouth, "Jesus is Lord," and believe in your heart that God raised him from the dead, you will be saved. For everyone who calls on the name of the Lord will be saved. (Romans 10:9,10,13)

Therefore, if anyone is in Christ, the new creation has come: The old has gone, the new is here! (2 Corinthians 5:17)

If you haven't already begun the ultimate adventure by becoming a follower of Jesus, take the first step today. NAIL IT DOWN! Document between you and the Lord that you have received Christ.

About the Author

Dr. Henry (Jay) Jacob Rupp has had an exciting life while riding the roller coaster of international ministry. Spiritual fruit is often out on the limb where there are lots of joys but challenges also. Dr. Rupp and his wife have served on short-term missions in Japan, Alaska, and Uganda before returning with their four children to East Africa as full-time missionaries working with Africa Inland Mission.

As a medical doctor, Dr. Jay was known for his loving, friendly manner with patients. While at Kijabe Hospital in Kenya, Dr. Rupp tutored and discipled medical students from around the world. After completing his studies at Bethel Seminary, he also served as Director of Chaplains at Kijabe Hospital.

More recently, Dr. Rupp has been Director of House Physicians at a St. Paul Hospital while he and Sandy have enjoyed ministering to international students at the University of Minnesota. For the last eight years, the Rupps have served as visiting chaplains ministering with Alaska natives at Alaska Christian College.

Dr. Rupp's faith has been stretched by working as the only doctor at a hospital along the pipeline in Alaska, driving through war-torn Uganda to do preventive healthcare, treating HIV/AIDS patients in Kijabe Hospital, supervising a possible Ebola outbreak, and suffering through several personal health crises. Dr. Rupp has written two other books: What if! and Christian Signboard Quotes.

In addition to his medical work, Dr. Rupp is a certified Bob Ross oil painting instructor, taxidermist, and potter. His driving passion is to grow closer to the Lord and enjoy Him forever; that is the "Ultimate Adventure!"

Made in the USA
Monee, IL
20 April 2021